Praise for *Why Men Win at Work*

Sunday Times Magazine: In the tradition of all the most efficient execs, Whitty-Collins sets out an almighty set of recommendations.

Hood Magazine: Gill Whitty-Collins is 2020's driving force in the fight against gender discrimination.

Kevin McCarten: A must-read for any manager/leader aiming or hoping to improve their business.

John Forsyth: Enlightening, thought provoking, and perhaps even life changing.

5* Amazon: Just finished reading #WhyMenWinAtWork and loved it. It's a book that wraps its arms passionately around the issue of gender inequality and draws you in. Gill Whitty-Collins shares her own insight and experience, along with that of many others, and paints a 360-degree picture of gender inequality in the workplace and why it is the way it is today.

5* Amazon: Before I read this book, I thought it is for people who work at companies. I was wrong. It is a 'must read' for everybody who work at companies, but it is much more than that. It needs to be read by parents, educators, students, people who work in media, and actually by everybody. Before I read this book, I thought it is another 'lean in' book, telling women to buckle up and putting all the responsibility on their shoulders. It is not. It does put the fair share on women's shoulders, but it does something much more than that. It makes the invisible dynamics visible; it brings the unconscious into consciousness, so that something can be done about it, rather than just saying superficially 'lean in'.

5* Waterstones: I found this a thoroughly enjoyable and insightful book – it's given me a lot to think about and a much,

much fuller understanding of why gender inequality exists in the workplace and what we can do about it.

5* Amazon: *Why Men Win at Work* is one of those rare business books that is easy to read, blends big data and personal experience, and most importantly leaves the reader with a clear set of recommendations to be the change they want to see in the world. Gill Whitty-Collins' direct and open style is perfect for the topic, challenging us all to relook at diversity and inclusion with fresh eyes. An essential read not just for those in business but also for parents, teachers and anyone with an interest in feminism and equality (that means everyone!).

5* Goodreads: Whitty-Collins sets out the hard-hitting truth about how gender equality really works in the corporate world. Unlike many books I have read on this subject, it is immensely readable and written from the perspective of a gender equality covert. The irony is that Gill was hugely successful in the corporate world and yet still felt compelled to write this book! You can feel her fury but it isn't directed at the male species – far from it. The author is empathetic to the fact that this is a tricky and complex area – it's not easy to fix but she does not shy away from hard-hitting recommendations and the need for urgent action. Read this and I defy you to look at the issues passively again.

5* Goodreads: This is an easy to read, eye opening book for anyone working in a corporate… A must read for anyone who suspects that there is gender bias, or is unaware that it still exists.

5* Waterstones: Gender balance is much-discussed and written about, and Gill Whitty-Collins' conversational and personal (often humorous) style brings new insight and powerful perspective to the debate… Having read this book, I will no longer look at feminism the same way and I am going to do my bit to make the world a better and more equal place for the next generation of men and women.

Why Men Win at Work
... and how we can make inequality history

GILL WHITTY-COLLINS

Luath Press Limited

EDINBURGH

www.luath.co.uk

First published 2020

ISBN: 978-1-913025-62-5

The paper used in this book is recyclable. It is made from
low chlorine pulps produced in a low energy, low emission
manner from renewable forests.

Printed and bound by ScandBook AB, Sweden

Typeset in 10.5 point Sabon by Main Point Books, Edinburgh

Contents

For my dad,
brother of three sisters,
father of three daughters
and the first 'femanist' I knew.

Preface

I COULDN'T HAVE written this book seven years ago. I wouldn't have even thought about writing it then. In fact, if someone had told me they were writing a book called *Why Men Win at Work*, I would have had no interest in it at all. If I had ever thought about it, I would have disagreed with the premise and maybe (probably) have got into an argument about it.

As the father of three girls, perhaps my poor dad had no choice but to believe in supporting girls and women because he was surrounded by us. To his huge credit, he embraced feminism and from as early as I can remember he never made us feel like we should do anything else but use our brains and work hard at school, get into a good university and get a good job that exercised our minds. Sadly, I did have girlfriends at school whose fathers didn't see girls the same way and parked all their paternal academic and career ambition with their sons. Not my dad though.

It also helped that I went to mixed schools where, thanks to a combination of hard work, sufficient intelligence and being famously well organised, I was usually top of the class or close to it. It really never occurred to me to question whether I was as good as or equal to a man. Nor did my time at the University of Cambridge give me any cause to ask gender inequality questions – I was a pretty average student there overall but was privileged to come across some truly brilliant minds which came in both the male and female form. Then it was on to a career at a big international company, where for the first 18 years I would have told you that, while of course I was aware of gender diversity issues, I had personally never been on the wrong end of them. I had never felt in any way held back as a woman and, to be honest, I didn't understand why people made an issue of it. I am rather ashamed to admit that I used to be one of those women who was rather arrogant and dismissive of women who talked about gender inequality, and believed the issue was that they were perhaps not strong enough and should 'man up' – or should I say, 'woman up'.

And then I saw it. And once I had seen it, I saw it everywhere.

Not the old-school 'bum tap in the photocopy room' kind. (Although I know this does still happen, along with its sinister digital age evolution of instant messenger stalking.) No, what I became aware of was the invisible kind. The unconscious kind of gender discrimination that is so embedded in our psyches that even good men with good intentions participate in and contribute to, men who would count themselves as unconditional believers in equality. The kind that is so unconscious and invisible that even women themselves sometimes don't see it happening and, even worse, contribute to it themselves. The kind that ultimately defeated me, when so many other barriers along the way had not – and has defeated, is defeating and will defeat many women in their careers if we continue to allow it to. The kind that is the real, underlying reason why women struggle to succeed and are so under-represented at the top levels in business and society.

And so now I have personally seen and understood it, I am livid, and I need to talk about it and do something about it. Why are men still winning at work? Why do we accept that we are living in a man's world where over 90% of all leadership positions in society and business are held by men and no progress is being made? We have seen that even a global pandemic couldn't shift us on gender equality – when I began writing this book a year ago it was clear we were stuck and since then we have even gone into reverse, thanks to Covid-19. Women have taken on even more of the burden of housework and childcare to the detriment of their careers and face a 'Not now dear' response to any attempt at equality or diversity discussions because this is not seen as a priority in a crisis. Yes,

I am livid and I have decided to talk about it, even though I know how unwelcome and resisted this subject can be by both men and women. I am talking about it because if we don't keep raising the issue and fighting it, the unconscious system will keep on running in its unconscious way and we will still be here, in the same place, in 100 years. Brilliant women will still be under-leveraged and will not attain the positions in business and in society that should be theirs. We simply cannot let this happen.

A few points before we get stuck in.

While I spent 25 years of my career at Procter & Gamble, my fight is against gender inequality, not against them. I believe they are one of the better companies in their intentions and efforts to drive gender diversity. The gender inequality issues I talk about are ones that are seen and experienced in companies and organisations everywhere.

In order to talk about this issue, I am sometimes going to need to make generalisations about 'men vs women'. I am very aware that we all sit on a spectrum of gendered behaviours, and on a spectrum of gender for that matter. There are men out there who will relate more to the 'female' characteristics I discuss and women who will relate more to the 'male' characteristics and people who will relate to other combinations of 'male' and 'female' characteristics. However, I need to make some generalisations about the way women are and the way men are, otherwise it isn't possible to talk about why women face inequality in business and society. And it is very important that we do talk about it.

I am also very aware that the gender diversity issue is only a subsection of the much broader equality and diversity issues that we face in our society. I will focus on gender inequality from the perspective of a cis white woman, because that is what I have experienced and understand, and will leave others who have the right knowledge and expertise to represent their experiences. I will say, however, that I believe that the interventions that will address the gender diversity issues I am raising will also go a long way to drive diversity and inclusion in general.

I must warn you that I am going to say some controversial things. I am going to say some things that you might not agree with or might not accept as real, or may believe are inflated versus reality. And you might get angry with what I will say. I know because this is what happens every time I discuss this subject, whether on a gender diversity panel or over a nice dinner and bottle of wine with friends. I have more to share than obvious points of view that everyone nods along with, otherwise I would not be wasting my time writing this book or asking you to waste your time reading it.

This book is not written by an academic researcher or HR expert, it is written based fundamentally on the personal experience of a female leader. While I cite independent sources for many of the things I share, others are based on my personal observations and hypotheses. All are founded, if not on something I have read or studied, on something I have actually seen, heard or felt. I believe my experience and the experiences of others are real and valid and I make no apology for it. Ultimately, I have no formal qualifications to be writing about this beyond the fact that I am a woman who has held a senior leadership role – and I believe this is as strong a qualification as any.

This is not another book written only for people who read feminist books and are passionate experts on gender diversity. It is also for the sceptics, for people who think they don't want or need to read a book on gender equality. If that's you, I hope I can persuade you that you do. This is also the opposite of one of those man-hating books, I have written it for men as much as I have for women. I believe that the majority of men are good and decent people who would never intentionally want to repress women, and that the issue for most men is simply a lack of awareness of gender equality issues and of how to address them. We need to end the 'women vs men' gender battles if we are going to drive equality.

Do I think gender inequality at work is the biggest problem

we have in the world today? No – it's not even the biggest problem women have, and it won't be as long as some women are being physically or sexually abused anywhere in the world. When one in three women will be raped or beaten in her lifetime[1] and women around the world are subjected to forced marriage, stoning, trafficking, female genital mutilation, acid attacks, 'honour' killings, slavery and servitude, gender inequality at work is a 'first world feminist problem' by comparison. These are much more important issues than the 'luxury gender issues' I will focus on, and these must be fought by every decent human being wherever they exist.

This book isn't about the hideous sexism or obvious sexism that everyone can see, which has been well covered by others. It is not about the awful things that the very small minority of men who are predators or misogynists consciously do to control and manipulate women. It is about the invisible and unwitting things that men do that may not come from bad intentions but that do have significant negative consequences. This book focuses on what happens when women have been lucky enough to avoid or survive physical or sexual abuse and have ploughed through all the crap – the sexual harassment in the street, at school, at college – and have strived to stop it undermining them and holding them back. It's about what happens when these women make it to work, in a good job, which they do very well. They work alongside men – men who, by and large, are decent, behave well, say the right things and wouldn't dream of making an overtly sexist comment, let alone do anything physically inappropriate. It's about all of the invisible, unconscious things they experience that will ultimately be what defeats most of these strong, intelligent, talented women.

Finally, for the record, I am a feminist, but this does not mean that I want women to rule the world. I do not believe that women are better or smarter than men. I simply believe that we are equal and that we should rule and run the world (and its businesses and organisations) together. But we are a long way from this, and I have insight to share as to why this is the case and what we need to do about it.

How this book works

ARE YOU SOMEONE who isn't really sure you need, or want, to read this book? Do you believe that gender inequality is no longer a big issue and there are other, more important priorities we should be focusing on? Then you are *exactly* someone who should be reading this book. Simply glance at some of the many statistics in **'Yes, it is an issue'**. I can guarantee that this chapter will show you how gender inequality is still a huge problem and why this issue is so important – and one that you want to immerse yourself in.

Are you like I was? A successful woman who was lucky not to be on the wrong end of gender inequality issues and wasn't interested in engaging in them? **'Do you have feminist phobia?'** I will go on to share some things you may not be aware of which will change your perspective on supporting other women and lay out how you can do this.

Are you a good, decent man who supports gender equality and believes you don't contribute to the issue, so you don't need to engage with it? Do you even worry that gender equality is a threat to you and your career? Perhaps you treat diversity and inclusion as a side enhancement, not as core to business success? If so, you're not in the small group of **'A few bad men'**, but you will come to see that men are winning at work and that this isn't actually in your best interests. You will agree that you do need to engage with the gender equality issue and be ready to sign up as a fully-fledged 'femanist'.

Is there a small part of you that, although you would never say it out loud, thinks that men get most of the top jobs because they deserve them? That **'Maybe men are just better?'** You will see the evidence that proves that there is no competence or intelligence gap between men and women. There is no logical reason for one gender to have a disproportionate share of key positions in business and society.

So why do men win at work and have most of the top jobs? Once all the questions and doubts about the gender equality cause have been addressed and everyone is fully on board, I will go beyond the facts and figures and delve into the underlying, unwitting and unconscious reasons that cause and perpetuate gender inequality. This includes 'The invisible power of culture (and other forces)', 'The science bit', 'The confidence vs competence equation' and 'Giving good meeting'.

It also includes 'The umbrella theory' where we will see how too many women believe in the myth of meritocracy and don't understand the need to invest in networking and self-marketing. We will also discuss the impact of unpaid labour (housework, childcare, etc) on women's ability to do this on top of a good job.

At this point, you may be asking yourself what about 'The women who win at work?'. Over 90% of the big jobs are held by men, but not 100%. I will introduce you to some exceptional women, the 'Super 7%', who have reached the highest levels in business. We'll explore their attitudes to work, men, family, childcare, dress codes and more, so you can understand what sets them apart.

When discussing gender inequality there is a lot of talk about 'sisterhood'. It's so important that women support each other and that, when they succeed, they put the ladder down for women to follow in their success. But there are not enough examples of this happening – 'Sisters are (not) doing it for themselves'. I will discuss why this is and how we all can and need to do more to remedy this.

Why can't women look at why men win at work and apply this to make them successful? In 'The cruel bit' we will look at why this just doesn't work and how there needs to be another way.

Having taken a journey through all of the things that drive gender inequality, we'll look at the bigger picture and ask, '**So why do men win at work?**' and '**What the hell are we going to do about it?**'. I will suggest interventions and initiatives to take, no matter if you are a parent, employer, manager, media-maker, woman or man, to sustainably drive equality and diversity in your world.

Yes, it is an issue

OVER THE YEARS I have had a lot of conversations with a lot of people about gender diversity and they virtually always start the same way. Sometimes I am talking with a woman who has been on the wrong end of gender inequality and is therefore painfully aware of the issue, 'gets it' and is keen to discuss it. But most of the time a gender equality discussion meets with one or more of the following responses:

1 I don't know why women are still making a thing about this, it's really not an issue anymore, certainly not where I work. Women are treated just the same as men. Sexism doesn't really exist anymore.

2 Women are equal now – more or less.

3 Frankly, I find it a bit embarrassing to complain about gender issues when we're so lucky compared with women even 50 years ago and women in other parts of the world who are dealing with real problems. With our nice jobs and big salaries, we have gilded lives really.

4 If I'm honest I think some women use it as an excuse. If they don't get the job or promotion they want, they blame gender inequality. Perhaps they should take a look at themselves and accept that they were just not as strong as the person who got it.

5 There aren't enough women with the right experience and credentials, that's the only reason men are getting most of the big jobs. We need to build the pipeline from the bottom.

6 Just putting women who are like men in senior jobs and on teams doesn't help anyone – some of them act more like men than the men, they are 'man-women'. That isn't the answer to driving diversity.

7 We shouldn't be talking just about gender diversity, we should be talking about diversity in general – the importance of diverse styles and thinking, which can come from men and women. (I would not argue with this either, but it rather misses the point that a group that is dominated by men and lacking women is also likely to be lacking in diversity of thought).

On the gender diversity front – yes, it is still an issue. Pleased as I am that we have made progress over the last 100 years and that women are now allowed to vote and leave the house on their own, what we have today is hardly what we could call equality for women. People see one woman get a CEO role or voted in as Prime Minister and they think it's job done. It's not. The progress we are seeing is at best very slow, at worst non-existent, and has us a very long way away from real equality – which, in case we are in any doubt, means 50% female.

At the Women's Equality Party Conference in 2018, Sandi Toksvig (the party's co-founder) brought the gender inequality issue alive in her hilarious way. She told us that of the FTSE 100 companies seven are run by women but 17 are run by men called John, with 14 by men called Dave.[1]

Let's look at some other, less amusing, gender equality facts.

Among the 2020 'Fortune 500' rankings of leading US businesses, the irritatingly celebratory *Fortune* headline of 'hits an all-time record' announced that 37, or 7%, have women CEOs (and not one has a black female CEO).[2] It is also worth noting that these women leaders are concentrated at the bottom of the Fortune 500, where the companies are smaller. Europe is even further behind, where less than 3% of Europe's S&P 500 companies have a woman CEO.[3]

One defence I often hear is that most women don't want to be a CEO because they have other priorities in life. While this may be true for some, don't try to tell me that 90% plus of men want to be CEO but only less than 10% of women do. In fact, 45% of women – versus 54% of men – say they would like to become a CEO.[4] Furthermore, at the beginning of their career, 43% of women – versus 34% of men – aspire to reach top management. (Although, after two or more years of experience, this is down to 16% for women, while for men the number remains the same.)[5]

We will discuss why this happens later, but nothing here indicates that only 7% of women want to get to CEO level, even once they have started to see the barriers they will face. And this is not just an issue of men versus women at CEO level. The Hampton-Alexander Review recently celebrated the FTSE 100 having 32.4% women in board positions (still a long way from 50%) with only 23.1% women in executive committee positions; and this is not on track to improve given that 68% of the new appointments are going to men.[6] Another stat to note, 66% of the HR executive positions are held by women but only 15% of the Finance Director (FD) positions. Only 25 of the FTSE 350 boards have appointed a woman as Chair. Two of the FTSE 100 boards and six of the executive committees are all-male, as are 38 of the FTSE 250 executive committees. Six FTSE 100 companies have no female directors.[7] Only 19% of US board positions are held by women[8] (somehow it seems more shocking to say that men hold 81% of board positions).

A 2018 McKinsey report found that 65% of all female executives are in non-management roles[9] and Grant Thornton's data from 2016 shows that women account for only 24% of US senior business roles.[10] A man is ten times more likely to make partner at a law firm and three times more likely at an accountancy firm, and only 10.5% of fund managers are female.[11]

Three per cent of global venture funding went to female-only founded start-ups in the year ending October 2019 and start-ups run by women get only 2% of US venture capital firms' investments, despite 39% of all privately held businesses being owned by women; interestingly, women-led funds also invest largely in men.[12] Even at the total workforce level there is a gender issue: in the US in 2000, 59.9% of women aged 15 and older were in the workforce; that fell to 58.6% by 2010 and 56.7% by 2015.[13]

At my previous company, which puts a lot of well-intended focus on driving gender equality, we nonetheless saw leakage of women at every level. Close to 50% of the recruits into the management entry level were women but by the second management level it was already dropping and by the third was down to around 40%. By Vice-President level, it was down to around 30% globally and lower in Europe. The United Nations (UN) has a similar leakage profile and say that it will take them 703 years to reach gender parity at the top level based on their past ten-year progress rates.[14]

When you step back and think about it, it's actually incredible that we allow this to be the case without working harder to understand it and to intervene. As Hanneke Faber, President of Europe for Unilever, dryly puts it, 'It's hard to believe women get more stupid over time.'

Women are also enormously under-represented in politics and law. According to the UN, as of October 2018, only 9% of Member States had a female Head of State or Government, and a 2020 World Economic report tells us that only 25% of parliamentary seats worldwide are held by women, slipping to only 21% at ministerial level.[15] Only ten countries have gender equal cabinets.[16]

Only 34% of UK MPs are female and there have been fewer female MPs in history than the number of men that hold seats in Parliament at one time.[17] Women currently hold only 27% of Cabinet positions, the lowest level since 2014 and only 7 out of 38 Lord Justices of Appeal and 19 out of 106 High Court Judges are women.[18]

In the US, four states have never sent a woman to the Senate or the House, only five states have a female governor and only 31 women have ever served as governor versus 2,317 men. Women hold 16.3% of seats in the House of Representatives and 16% of seats in the Senate. A record 110 women now serve in Congress, which represents a pitiful fifth of seats.[19]

Only 10% of Japan's legislators, senior officials and managers are women.[20]

The lack of women in leadership in politics is particularly critical as it both illustrates the extent of the gender gap and it plays a major role (perhaps one of the most important of all) in creating and maintaining it. According to the World Bank, only six countries currently give women and men equal rights. In the average nation, women receive just three-quarters of the legal rights that men do.[21] As Caroline Lucas MP said:

> If more women were here [in parliament], it would
> be more likely that the issues that are demonstrably
> unequal in terms of their impact on women would be
> picked up and stopped... the policies coming out of
> this place would be fairer to women.[22]

It was also noted by many during the Covid-19 crisis that some of the UK plans, for example on school opening, had serious flaws that had not been caught because women's perspective was missing in their development.

The gender diversity issue in the media arena is also important. A Women in Journalism study found that four out of five front-page stories were written by men, with 84% of those stories being dominated by a male subject.[23] One in five solo presenters on UK radio is female (only one in eight during peak time). Women make up only 24% of people heard, read about or seen in newspapers, television and radio news. A pathetic 5% of sports media coverage in the UK is devoted to women's sport and comedy shows such as *Mock the Week* have been criticised for 'gender tokenism' with their male-dominated panels.[24]

It's the same story in film: women make up only 21% of all film-makers, and in the 92 year history of the Oscars, only five women have been nominated for the Best Director Award (only one has ever won it, Kathryn Bigelow) and only 14% of all nominations have gone to women.[25] A woman has never won the Best Picture Award and Jane Campion is the only woman to have won the Cannes Film Festival's Palme d'Or in its 72-year history. Perhaps it is not surprising then that male actors spend 100% more time on screen in films than females do, they also have 69% of the speaking roles, with only 23% of films featuring a female protagonist.

Research from the Geena Davis Institute on Gender in Media found that, from 2006 to 2009, not one female character was depicted in G-rated family films in the field of medical science, as a business leader, in law, or politics[26] and that in the top 100 US family films of 2019, male leads outnumber female leads two to one.[27] They saw the same issue in advertising: based on their analysis of over 2.7 million YouTube ads from 2015 to 2019, they saw female characters 44% of the time but only 29% of the time in a business and industrial context, with men having 50% more speaking time and more likely to be shown working and in leadership positions.[28]

Female characters, meanwhile, are significantly more likely to wear revealing clothing and to be shown in the kitchen, shopping or cleaning. Perhaps this is not entirely surprising when we learn that, globally, 89% of creative directors are men.[29]

When we watch a film or TV show with our 'gender glasses'

on, we start to notice that we are constantly served up male-created media full of male-driven stories and characters. Caroline Criado Perez's *Invisible Women* brilliantly documents the extent to which the male experience has come to be seen as universal and the female perspective is excluded and what we see is, at best, a limited, one-dimensional representation of women and, at worst, a damaging one. This is critical because it is proven that we are all greatly influenced by what we see on screen and around us – if we see men in the boardroom and women in the kitchen it affects how we all perceive women and their role in society.

Haley Swenson, a fellow at New America, observed in her response to Pew Research Center's study (which calculated gender representation in top Google image search results) that Google significantly under-represents women as managers and chief executives:[30]

> We know that what people see affects what they
> perceive to be normal, and that in turn affects
> behaviour... If you don't think it's normal for a person
> like you to do a certain job, then you just don't do
> that... one of the things that drives sexual harassment
> is men in those jobs perceive women as infringing in a
> space that's supposed to be theirs.[31]

We could ask Katrín Jakobsdóttir, the Prime Minister of Iceland, about this. As she was about to take the podium to deliver a speech, she was asked where the Prime Minister of Iceland was.[32] She clearly didn't look like the kind of person (read correct gender) who would or could do that job. One of the key problems is that so few of us are actually aware of the extent to which we are being influenced by the media and images over time – the impact is largely unconscious for us. Seeing their own experience and identity reflected back at them is something men take for granted and they are not conscious of the very different experience women have in this context. As

Laura Bates puts it in *Everyday Sexism*:

> For a white, middle-aged, middle-class man who sees
> his own face staring back out of every page, every
> news bulletin, every panel show, it must be difficult to
> imagine being one of many regular women looking
> through paper after paper, magazine after magazine,
> watching film after film and rarely catching a glimpse
> of yourself.[33]

What is perhaps even more worrying is the 'invisible knowledge' that is being developed by artificial intelligence based on newspapers, magazines and literature from across time – the computers that are making decisions for us are being taught to be biased towards men and against women.

This over-representation of men in the media has a significant impact on how we perceive women, especially when combined with the role models we see in CEO and senior management roles, politics, the justice system or even in education (only one in five UK professors and only one in seven of the teaching staff at the University of Cambridge are women, for example).[34] Only half of Italian women and 40% of Japanese women believe a woman is an electable leader. 'Women should concentrate on the household while men work.'[35] So we are not only facing a huge gender gap in the here and now, we are facing a self-fulfilling prophecy that will never unravel itself unless there is radical change. We need to break the cycle or we will never see women in the roles we should see them in, and to do this the representation of women needs to change – both in the important roles they play in society and in the images we project of them.

The good news is that this does and will work both ways. Indira Gandhi became Prime Minister of India in 1966 and when her term ended in 1977 89% of Indian women believed a woman was an electable leader.[36] After eight years of Iceland's Vigdís Finnbogadóttir's presidency, children under eight thought only a woman could be President![37]

I think we are all aware of the gender pay gap. The UK's national average gap is 17.3%.[38] The BBC was put in the spotlight in 2017 when female presenters, including Sue Barker, Fiona Bruce and Clare Balding, and Carrie Gracie in 2019, decided to complain publicly. Good for them, but in fact the BBC are far from the worst offenders. In 2019, women who work for the BBC had an average salary of 6.7% lower than their male peers,[39] while at the Independent Television Network (ITN) it was 15%.[40] Women are making what men made in 2006 and statisticians estimate that, at this rate, the gap won't close until 2186.[41] It is of course not just a UK issue – the average gender pay gap in Europe is 16%[42] (and I have seen a number as high as 29% in one company); French women's salaries are 23.8% below men's;[43] in America, full-time working women make 83% of what full-time working men make[44] and, on average, all women make 79 cents for every dollar men make;[45] and Japanese women's average income is 73% of men's.[46] (In the finance sector it is only 55%.[47]) The pay gap is everywhere.

It starts with the first job after graduation (20% of men earned over £30,000 after their degree but only 8% of women did and, in law, the women's graduate salaries averaged £20,000, some £8,000 less than the men's)[48] and it continues, with women receiving lower average bonuses; women's starting salaries are 6% less, bonuses 19% less.[49] As a result, we see that the average female executive earns £423,000 less over her lifetime than a man with an identical career path[50] and we should not, I suppose, be surprised to learn that only 9% of the world's 1,125 billionaires are women.[51]

The gender issue is not only showing up once women are working for a company; it is there at the recruitment stage too. One experiment showed that when hiring researchers for a job, men were twice as likely to be hired than women.[52] In another study, thousands of phantom student emails were sent to professors at academic institutions requesting a meeting.

87% of the men got a yes and only 62% of the women.[53] Cornell University sent out 1,276 fake resumes and found that the most desirable applicants were men with kids and the least desirable were – wait for it – women with kids.[54]

So yes, gender diversity is an issue. It is happening. It is a problem for all of us – and our companies, organisations, societies and countries would be much better places if it were not. It is time to stop with the 'maze of denial'.[55] Not all of us see or experience gender inequality as strongly or clearly as others and many (men and women) don't want to acknowledge or talk about it. But nobody can look at this data and not see that gender inequality is an issue and that this is a man's world.

2

Do you have feminist phobia?

ONE OF THE things that most frustrates me is when women themselves are in denial about the gender diversity issue, have 'feminist phobia' and fiercely resist calling themselves a feminist or being seen as one by others. How often do we hear women say, 'Well I wouldn't go as far as to call myself a feminist but...'? If you are one of these women, I can only assume that you must not then realise that the definition of a feminist is simply: 'A person who believes in the social, political and economic equality of the sexes.'[1]

I doubt there is a woman out there who would not say that they are a feminist based on this definition. However, many women do struggle with being seen as a feminist because of the negative associations that have been wrongly attached to feminism over time. The baggage has done the gender equality cause no favours. While there is nothing in this definition about female superiority or supremacy and nothing about hating men, sadly many people see these things as intrinsic to feminism and, as a result, they dislike and fear it. Especially in the corporate world, many women find it easier and smoother to avoid labelling themselves with something that will be viewed negatively by men, and especially by men who have power over their jobs and careers. As Helena Morrissey says in *A Good Time to Be a Girl*:

> Some... did not want to be part of a specific women's initiative [the '30% Club'], expressing concerns about

how that would be perceived by their male peers...
they do not want to be seen as flying the women's
flag... real businesswomen should be focusing on real
business issues, rather than on women.[2]

Some women believe that they will benefit from avoiding the association because of the perception that only 'weak' women can't handle themselves in the workplace or the world and need to blame gender issues when they don't succeed, so they choose to position themselves as 'above this'. This perception of feminism is by no means imagined – a study in 2016 showed that the performance of women who engaged in diversity efforts was rated lower.[3] When Helena Morrissey established the '30% Club' in 2010, with the aim of achieving 30% female representation on FTSE 100 boards, she was accused of 'destroying British business' and told 'how difficult, wearisome and often discouraging' her efforts were.[4] Even Australian Prime Minister Julia Gillard was accused by the Australian media of 'playing the gender card' and told that she had 'demeaned every woman in this Parliament' when she raised gender diversity issues.[5]

I saw this distancing from feminism very clearly in the senior women at my previous company during a gender diversity training day for our senior managers in Europe. Now bear in mind that this was a training investment by the company with, I assume, the intent of understanding and tackling gender issues. And yet I felt I was the only woman there who was willing to speak out openly about what I as a woman felt and saw in what was a largely male team. Beyond a few tentative comments (that were met with silence and lack of comprehension by the men), the other women stayed quiet. It was clear that they didn't want to be associated with the gender issue and, moreover, that they didn't want to be associated with me or with what I was saying about gender inequality in case it reflected badly on them. In truth, they were not wrong to be concerned about how they might be seen if they spoke up – I was told at one point in my career by a very senior man that I should 'tone it down on the women stuff' as it made me look weak and self-serving. But by the time of this training day, I had reached a senior and visible enough level to be in a position to take on the cause for the more junior women and drive change, or so I believed. However, it seems women can't ever reach a senior enough level to be able to do that. Even female CEOs admit to steering clear of it for fear of not being seen as focusing on 'real business issues'. (If you are asking yourself if I toned it down, of course I didn't!)

What is terrifying is that even young girls have learnt not to speak up in front of boys about the sexism they experience for fear of how they may be perceived. Laura Bates talks about schoolgirls she spoke with who

> are incredibly eloquent and insightful in conversation
> with me... And yet later, during a similar discussion
> with their whole year group, they clam up
> completely... in front of their male peers... they go
> unchallenged at every stage.[6]

This is a sad mini-version of what I have seen so many times in women aged 45+ in very senior management positions – no wonder, we had already learnt our lessons on the safest way to behave and speak in front of men when we were at school.

Even worse though than women staying quiet on this issue are women who actively come out on the side against women. One example of this was when LBC radio presenter Julia Hartley-Brewer covered the Lord Rennard sexual harassment allegations in 2013 and said, 'Throughout this case I've been quite disgusted by how pathetic [the female victims have] come across.'[7]

For the most part though, we see women staying quiet about gender diversity issues. They avoid drawing attention to themselves and their issues as women and instead to try to fit in and side with, or at least not irritate, men. I recently heard one man say of a woman he works with that 'She's a jolly good chap', which made me almost want to scream thinking of how this woman must feel she needs to behave and what she must ignore and negate in order to be seen as 'one of the lads'.

So, to the women out there – while I completely understand these are coping mechanisms in an unequal world, we are not 'jolly good chaps' and we have a responsibility to ourselves and to other women. We need to have the courage to say, 'I am a feminist' and, when necessary, to educate others on what that means. You will not come across many people who disagree with social, political and economic equality of the sexes – and, if you do, I would suggest they are not someone whose opinion you should care about!

I witnessed an example of some vintage female denial of gender diversity issues on a board skills training course I recently attended. It started when we were arriving and gathering on the first morning. Not everyone was in the room yet and at that point we had nine female participants and one man, who asked in jest if he had inadvertently signed up for a women-only course. We all laughed, and I said:

> You're getting a little taste of how women feel, we're usually completely outnumbered in most meetings we attend.

Most of the women smiled and nodded in recognition except one, who said:

> Frankly, I don't know why people still make a thing about gender, I don't think it's really a problem in this day and age.

It was fascinating to see how quickly and clearly this woman wanted to deny the gender issue and completely disassociate herself from it in order, based on my take, to 'fit in' and to be viewed more positively by the man in the group.

It didn't stop there though, and it didn't stop with this one woman. After dinner that evening, the discussion turned to gender inequality and one man (who had not arrived in time for the morning exchange) also said that he didn't understand why we still needed to talk about gender diversity because he didn't see it at all in his company or on his team. Now this is something I fully expect to hear from a man, and I will discuss why later on in the book. What surprised me was the response from a number of the women in the group. I very politely pointed out (because I believe we have a responsibility not to stay quiet and let these things be said without challenge) that there is an enormous amount of data to show that there is very much still a gender inequality issue. One woman passionately agreed with the man that it is not an issue anymore. Another woman at my table told me that she had never experienced it as a problem in her long career and that she believed that women who complain about it are just using it as an excuse because they are not 'strong' enough to perform and compete with the men. There was not a single woman in the room, apart from myself, who was willing to acknowledge it as a real issue, let alone as something they had personally witnessed or experienced. These women absolutely did not want to be associated with gender issues – they preferred to be seen as 'one of the boys'.

This is by no means an isolated experience, but it is one of the most extreme examples of female denial that I have seen. I was not only extremely frustrated by it; I was very upset. While I personally was not on the wrong end of gender inequality or diversity issues when I was younger and more junior in my career, I find it difficult to believe that these women, who were all experienced and at senior levels, had truly never experienced these issues – and, if they had, I do not think it is acceptable to collude with men by denying it and pushing it underground. I raise my eyebrows when I hear someone like Amaia Gorostiza of Spanish football club SD Eibar, saying:

I have never been treated differently on my visits to other stadiums and I have always worked in male-dominated environments.[8]

As a female CEO of a football club, really...? Even if these women have by some miracle managed to avoid the gender issue throughout their careers, I don't like to see the experience of other women being negated and denied (or of any person experiencing inequality). There is a world and workplace full of women telling us that gender inequality has negatively affected them, so please let's listen to and respect them.

Let's remember that gender issues are not just about overt sexist actions and comments, objectification or worse. If you haven't been sexually harassed, told by your boss that you would lose your job if you didn't sleep with him, had your body commented upon by a man in your office, or been verbally insulted or overtly patronised – then that is good news, some women have unfortunately had to endure these things but thankfully most have not. But to any women out there who say they have not experienced gender inequality, I would ask this:

Have you sat in a meeting watching the men hold the floor for ages and waiting for your chance to speak but struggling to get a word in?

Then, when you finally do get the chance to speak, do you feel under pressure to make your point quickly because you know you won't be allowed much time before someone cuts in (and knowing afterwards that you didn't make your point as strongly and convincingly as you could have)?

Or have you been interrupted in the middle of your point, even though you only had the floor for about 30 seconds and one of the men delivered an impromptu ten-minute, five-point monologue earlier?

Have you ever made a point or suggestion that was ignored or barely acknowledged and then repeated later in the meeting by a man, at which point it becomes a brilliant idea and every-one starts engaging enthusiastically with it?

And did you ever get to the point where you stopped bothering to try to contribute anymore in a meeting you attend regularly because nobody was really listening to or registering what you were saying, so there didn't seem to be much point?

Or, did you ever lose out on a new role or promotion to a man who wasn't as capable or competent as you? Did you ever in your whole career see any of these things happen to other women?

If you can say yes to any of these questions, then you have experienced the gender diversity issue. There is a 'pyramid' of visible to invisible dynamics which leads to what I call the 'Gender Maturity Pyramid' for the desired end state.

The Gender Maturity Pyramid
Design by Sofía Lahmann

Many women, thankfully, have not experienced or witnessed the bottom of the pyramid – the visible and purely sexist stuff – and many work for very good organisations that make great efforts to support women through maternity and parenting, so they may believe that gender diversity is not a relevant issue anymore or for them. However, I believe most women, if not all, are being affected by the top of the pyramid issues that I am personally focused on (although to reiterate, the 'bottom of the pyramid' issues and the women facing them must be our highest priority where they exist).

I know that there will still be a few of you out there who are genuinely feeling that you have had a positive experience and have not come across any of the gender pyramid issues, even those at the top of the pyramid. As I said earlier, I get it – I had the same mindset a few years ago when I was at a less senior level (even up to Director). I'm ashamed to admit that I was one of the women who saw myself as 'strong' and above all that and not affected by it and who couldn't imagine a man being able to hold me back. So I'm not in a position to blame anyone for not seeing the issue – it was only once I reached a senior management level that was male-dominated that I started to see and experience it.

It is possible that you are not even noticing that you are experiencing it – as Laura Bates says in *Everyday Sexism*, many women see and accept these things as

just part of life – or, rather, part of being a woman... women become so accustomed to experiencing gender-based prejudice that they almost fail to even register it anymore.[9]

Or it may also be that you are still relatively young and have not really hit this yet, but I'm afraid to say that if you keep progressing and getting promoted and the world continues to be as it is now, then you will – so don't be like I used to be and believe that you won't. As one executive who spent 30 years in Fortune 500 companies says, 'Before heading to the c-suite (CEO, CMO, CFO level), I didn't feel I was handicapped at all.'[10] If there *is*, though, a female CEO or Board Director out there who really feels she has not faced gender issues and has never needed to adapt to male behaviours to fit in and succeed, please get in touch – if you exist, you are our role model and we need to prototype you! But above all, if you are lucky enough to be one of the rare women who have a positive personal story as a woman in the workplace, please don't negate the experience of those women who have not and who have lived through or are living with gender diversity issues. Please be aware, listen and learn.

3

A few bad men

ONE OF MY biggest hopes for this book is that it is read by men and makes a difference to how they understand gender inequality – and therefore to how they respond to it. And so, before we go any further, I would like to set a few things straight with the men out there.

I know many men who will not buy or open this book because they believe it is not something they want or need to read and I know that some of you who have started to read are still not sure if it is for you and if you should carry on. Some of you, like some women, will have 'feminist phobia' because of the aggressive, man-hating baggage the term 'feminism' has had attached to it – and which has nothing to do with it. Feminism is purely and simply about believing in equality: I am a feminist, but I am not, have never been, and never will be, a man-hater. I cannot say strongly enough that man-hating actions and words from anyone are the opposite of helpful to the gender equality cause, so please don't fall into the trap of assuming feminists are man-haters. I know that some women, in their passionate fight for gender equality, do feel the need to project an image of men as the sinister, repressive enemy. Understandably, this makes you feel defensive and does not encourage you to want to support women or this fight. More importantly, it isn't true, and it isn't fair to men. As with everything and everyone in this life, male characteristics are on a spectrum. At one extreme of this, yes, there is a very small percentage, 'a few bad men', who are sexist, misogynists and know it (I leave you to work out why I like to call these men 'the Trumpets') – but these men are rare and do not represent the vast majority of men. Further, there is an absolutely tiny percentage of men that have actually raped or physically assaulted a woman – and these men are abhorred as much by other men as they are by women and shouldn't be grouped and labelled along with them. To do so is, as Laura Bates puts it, 'deeply insulting to the vast majority of men, who are perfectly able to control their sexual desires'.[1]

At the other extreme of the spectrum we have what I call the 'femanists'; another tiny percentage. These are the men who really get it, they see the gender diversity issue, they understand it, they really care about it and they contribute to addressing it. The best example of a 'femanist' I have ever had the privilege to meet is clinical psychologist and consultant John Van Vleet. He has an incredible insight into and comprehension of the things men do, consciously and unconsciously, that create barriers for women and hold them back. He works tirelessly across the world to train men on gender inequality and on how to work on it in their businesses, organisations and lives. If only there were more Johns working on gender inequality – and more people signing up for his training!

And in between these two very small percentages ('A few bad men' and the 'femanists') at each end of the spectrum, we have the rest of the men – 90% plus of them, the huge majority. They are not misogynists; they are not sexist – they are good men with good intentions who respect women and believe that they are supporting them. But they don't realise they are often getting it wrong. They don't mean to, they are unaware that they are unwittingly supporting gender inequality because, as we will discuss, so much of this issue is driven by unconscious bias and invisible factors.

One thing we all need to remember is that, in most cases, men are not aware of the issues and restraints women are facing simply because *they are not women*. We are all, I think, aware in some way of Donald Rumsfeld's concept that 'we don't know what we don't know'[2] – well men don't know what they don't know either. It should be expected that a man cannot know and understand the experience of a woman, no matter how decent a man he is and how good his intentions are. Of course men don't get gender equality in the same way women do and women shouldn't be angry with them for that. The huge majority of men are not sinister or malicious, they are for the most part just simply oblivious.

This is not, however, an excuse for men not to take responsibility for their lack of awareness of what it is to live life and do a job as a woman. You don't know what you don't know, but that doesn't mean you can't try to better understand or empathise with the female situation. That means being on high alert and watching and listening extra carefully to learn and develop. I have come across a few men who are very aware of the barriers women face and of their male privilege. These men try as best they can not to misuse it, but many men do not even notice male privilege, and, for some men, it has even become an entitlement. Whoever was responsible for the ill-conceived TV show *A Black Woman Took My Job* certainly missed the point on many levels – er, excuse me, 'my' job? A popular little 'funny' some men at my ex-company would say was 'I'd like to be reborn as a black lesbian woman so I can get promoted.' If anyone is reading this thinking it is easier for a black lesbian woman to get a promotion ahead of a white heterosexual man, then you really need to keep reading – and I hope you will feel very differently by the end. Recall there are only 37 female CEOs of the Fortune 500 and not a single one of these is a black woman.

As we are talking about excuses and not hiding behind a lack of awareness, here's a quick rant about something that I believe has provided the perfect hiding place for some men from gender issues.

The #MeToo movement has been extremely important in shining a light on to the bottom of the pyramid issues. It has created a space for people to share experiences they previously felt they could not and it has been a huge movement for change. It is appalling to know that women (or anyone, for that matter) have been sexually harassed in their work and pressured into sex. This must be exposed and the 'few bad men' who do these things must be stopped and severely dealt with. The #MeToo movement has focused on dangerous, manipulative men who are guilty of committing criminal acts but thankfully this is only relevant to a tiny minority of men. One unintended consequence of this focus is that it has given men who aren't guilty of the hideous bottom of the pyramid stuff the opportunity to feel complacent, even smug and to disengage from gender equality issues: 'I don't sexually harass or abuse or manipulate women so I'm above all this.' By only focusing the discussion on these #MeToo gender issues, we lose men from the conversation. Most men don't do these things, they think they're irrelevant to them and so they may feel they can excuse themselves from the whole gender equality issue.

#MeToo has shown that we are years (decades even) behind where we should be in the gender equality conversation. We should not need to be dealing with and discussing 'casting couch' issues well into the 21st century, these should have been fixed and forgotten years ago. But they haven't been and so we are being forced (rightly) to focus on these discussions and thus diverted and distracted from having the 'top of the gender diversity pyramid' discussions we need to have. We need to be talking about unconscious bias and discrimination from decent men that is also preventing equality and holding us back. Let's not box ourselves in by only discussing a minority of men who treat women as sex objects, let's talk about how the majority of men are unwittingly stopping women becoming leaders.

So, to all the men out there – please don't hide behind #MeToo and use it as an opportunity to avoid the gender equality conversation. You are, I'm sure, no Weinstein or Epstein and are well above these bottom of the pyramid issues, but *no* man is above contributing to gender inequality.

At this stage I am going to make the assumption that you

are with me – you are one of the majority of good men who has good intentions and who is willing to accept that you have the privilege of being male in our society and may sometimes – unconsciously and unintentionally – think, say or do things that create barriers for women. You, no doubt, believe we are making progress and are possibly one of the 72% of male company directors who believe that too much attention is paid to gender diversity, or one of the 49% of men globally who think the workplace is a level playing-field for men and women (only 31% of women agree).[3] Or perhaps you are one of the 67% of men who believe companies and boards will just naturally become more diverse over time.[4] You may feel you have more pressing things to focus on. The question then is why should you do anything to help change things? Why should you care? Why give up your male privilege? Why should you help women succeed? Surely that would be like giving up the front row seats at the game – and not just for one game, for every game, home and away, every season, forever. Why should you sign up to be a 'feminist'?

I get that if we want you to help and support women in this (and we really, really do) then you need to understand why gender equality is a good thing and, specifically, why it is in your interest. So, boys, it's time for the sales pitch.

The easy assumption is that if women win, men lose. In fact, there is a very strong data-based case to show that this isn't true, and that gender equality is a good thing for everyone.

A couple of years ago, I was lucky to have the chance to attend a speech given by Dr Michael Kimmel – he's been called 'the world's biggest male feminist' by *The Guardian*,[5] and I say, can there be a greater compliment to a man than this? His research has shown that when men share the housework and childcare, their children do better at school and are healthier and happier, their wives are happier, the men are happier and – wait for it – they have more sex.[6]

Perhaps I can just close my sales pitch there. But I won't because there is so much more. Not only does gender equality benefit the family, it benefits society as a whole. It has been shown that more equal nations do better on virtually all measures. In Sweden, the average life expectancy is an impressive 83 years,[7] in a country where women hold almost half (47%) of all seats in parliament (versus 16% in the US and 32% in the UK)[8] and 51% of all professional and technical positions. The Women's World Index found that by bringing paid parental leave and healthcare for women to 'best in class', the United States could increase its gross domestic product (GDP) by 35%.[9] McKinsey found that closing the gender gap in the workforce is worth $2.1 trillion growth in the US, +1% GDP growth per year, 6.4 million more jobs[10] and could add $28 trillion to the global GDP, nearly the size of the US and Chinese economies combined.[11] As always, Sandi Toksvig said it well at the 2018 Women's Equality Party Conference: 'Women's equality has the potential to transform our economy and our lives.'[12] Michael J Silverstein and Kate Sayre, in *Women Want More,* similarly said:

> The rise of women... holds within it what may be the largest commercial opportunity we have ever seen or will see in our lifetime.[13]

In between the two ends of the spectrum between family and nation, gender equality is a proven positive driver for companies and thus a positive impact for everyone – in Dr Kimmel's words, 'Gender equality is good for business... not a zero sum game, we make the pie bigger.'[14] One of the most important things I would say to men is this is not charity – this is business. Numerous Goldman Sachs studies have shown that gender diverse companies outperform competitors on every key measure.[15] A 2011 Catalyst study showed that companies with three or more female directors achieved significantly better financial results and that the companies with the most female board directors outperformed those with the least by 16% in sales and 26% in ROI.[16] New Australian research based on six years of companies' reporting to the federal Workplace Gender Equality Agency has established that companies who appointed a female CEO increased their market value by 5%.[17] The top 50 companies have women in 33% plus of their board seats, and large companies that have boards with three or more women tend to be more profitable, have a higher return on asset and better market performance.[18] This could in part be related to the fact that women make up half of the population. Yang Mianmian of Qingdao Refrigerator General Factory believes having women in a business is critical because they bring insights and knowledge that men miss: 'Being a woman in home appliances helps a lot. I am the designer and manufacturer and also the user.'[19] The fact that, as a woman, she is the primary user of the home appliances is something we will address later.

In 2018, McKinsey found that companies with gender diversity delivered 21% more profitability. They also found that companies with more women on executive teams were 27% more likely than those with the least women to be leading their industry in value creation and profit ability. In addition, McKinsey revealed that leading companies have a higher share of executive women in line roles – whereas companies in the 4th quartile on diversity are more likely to underperform versus their industry peers.[20]

A GALLUP® 2014 study examined data from more than 800 business units from two companies, one representing retail and the other hospitality. They found that gender diverse business units in the retail company had 14% higher average comparable revenue than less diverse business units and the hospitality company showed 19% higher average quarterly net profit than less diverse business units.[21] The positive effect on business practices has also been consistently shown. For example, firms with a higher percentage of women board directors and led by women Chairs were less likely to commit fraud or violate security regulations.

Russell Reynolds Associates revealed the power for

businesses of diverse and inclusive cultures led by leaders (men and women) with natural 'diversity aware' traits.[22] They conducted extensive Diversity and Inclusion (D&I) research, asking more than 1,800 leaders globally about their organisations' D&I strategies and practices. They saw that teams with 'diversity aware', open-minded leaders tend to see better outcomes, including greater job satisfaction, sense of belonging and employee loyalty – when employees have positive working relationships with their leaders and feel they can act authentically in the workplace (no matter how 'diverse' they may feel), they are more likely to contribute at higher levels than others and improve the organisation's performance. As a result, these teams produce innovative ideas with stronger risk management and more readiness to disrupt, transform and focus on the future. When surveyed these teams reported that inclusive leaders empowered their teams to perform at a higher level (92% vs 26%); facilitated high quality decision-making (90% vs 24%), higher levels of innovation (90% vs 30%) and agility (91% vs 29%); and enabled them to manage risk better (91% vs 34%). One specific example was Caterpillar HR Director Latasha Gillespie, who organised teams with a focus on diversity in gender, geographic background, generations, language and function. The teams generated incremental sales results ahead of the businesses using traditional methods.

The performance data differences are not marginal between teams that are diverse and those that are not and, importantly, it takes an inclusive leader to create and develop an inclusive, diverse team. As many organisations undervalue inclusive leadership, they miss important opportunities to promote leaders who have these skills. Only 40% of executives believe their leadership is held accountable for fostering an inclusive culture and only 35% said their leadership considers inclusive behaviours as promotion criteria for leaders.[23] So here we have a classic self-fulfilling prophecy at work – inclusive leadership drives diversity and diversity drives performance, but inclusive leaders need to be born and raised somewhere and this is extremely unlikely to happen in a non-diverse culture. This means that those who want stronger teams and better results (and is there anyone out there who doesn't want that?) need to take the fastest possible route to create a diverse team, including identifying, nurturing and promoting those (men and women) who demonstrate the inclusive leadership behaviours that will drive this – these are the ones who should be winning at work.

There is almost endless data on the power of diverse teams to drive stronger performance and, specifically within this, on the relative strength of gender diverse teams. As Anita Woolley and Thomas Malone laid out in the *Harvard Business Review* in June 2011, based on their research assigning intelligence tasks to teams:

> The only variable that predicted the success of a team was the inclusion of women... If a group includes more women, its collective intelligence rises.[24]

The evidence of the truth of this is everywhere. It starts early too – studies show that in high school, the classrooms with the best academic achievement were consistently those that had a higher percentage of girls.

Let's be absolutely clear here – nobody is saying that women are more intelligent than men but rather that having women on the team increases the *collective* intelligence of the team (and, as Woolley and Malone found, it even alters the collective thought process and changes male behaviour positively).[25] Nobody is saying that women are more insightful than men, but rather that they bring different insights that men may miss. Nobody is saying that women are superior to men, but rather that a team with a balance of men and women will be superior to a male-dominated one. In the words of Emmanuelle Quiles, Présidente Diréctrice Générale of Janssen France, 'quand on exclut une population, on exclut une partie de notre capacité à créer de la valeur' (translated as 'when we exclude a population, we exclude part of our ability to create value').[26] William White's 'Groupthink' concept from 1952 is hardly new and is embraced by Rightmove's ex-Chair Scott Forbes, who says that 'diversity immunises a board against groupthink'– yet still most organisations and companies are set up without sufficient diversity to avoid it. Surely, logically, as Dr Scott Page says, 'it's clear that an organisation wouldn't want, say, all white men'[27] – but this is pretty close to what we actually have in many organisations. Ultimately, all companies should want diversity of thought and Andy Haldane, Chief Economist at the Bank of England, gives us a good illustration of how to think differently about diversity. While recruiting he saw that Candidate A got 8/10 in the screening test and Candidate B got 4/10. But he concluded that B, not A, should be hired. This was because candidate B's correct four answers included the two that A got wrong; he knew that what was needed was 'the best person to complete the team.'[28]

This is not about women versus men. Any team that is not diverse is missing out, including a female-dominated one. This is about the importance of diversity of thought, skills and approach in the building of superior teams, businesses and societies. And surely everyone would choose to be on a superior, more intelligent, more insightful, more skilled team, especially with the knowledge that any company that is not developing its collective human intelligence will be less likely to succeed.

In fact, the gender gap is a double whammy hit. Number one, we are not leveraging the women who could strengthen the team and the results. Number two, we're not stretching the men we have as much as we could because we are making it too easy for them to get the jobs and promotions by handicapping their female competition.

So, boys, I'm not asking you to care about this just because you are a good man with a wife, mother, or daughter who you love, or because it's the right and fair thing to do. I'm not asking you to feel sorry for women and to do this to be 'nice' to them. Don't do this for women, do it for you. I know it may not feel appealing to sacrifice your male privilege – but in reality, it is not actually a sacrifice. I put this question to you: do you want to win at work and continue encouraging male dominance if it means your business will perform worse than if it was gender diverse? Do you want gender inequality, or would you prefer to be in a more successful company where men and women have a fair share of the roles? If you want your business and thus you personally to win (and of course you do), all of the evidence says that this really means that you want to *stop seeing* men win at work. You want to be part of a more diverse, more productive, more successful, gender equal company. So, the question is really how we can say that men are winning at work if this means women losing out on their share of roles cause the results to be weaker than they should be. Surely nobody is winning from that.

I hope it's clear that none of this is about hating or undermining men. Nobody is accusing you of being a bad person and nobody is trying to give anything to women at your expense. You have nothing to lose from supporting gender equality and becoming a fully-fledged 'femanist' – in fact, you have as much to gain as anyone.

4

Maybe men are just better?

SO, EVERYONE, WE have established that men *are* winning at work and that gender diversity *is* an issue. Now we need to stop denying that there's a problem and start truly tackling it. But before we answer the key question (*why* are men more successful and why do men win at work?), I think we need to put a question on the table that I know some of you (men and women) have asked yourselves, even if you have never dared to say it out loud. The question is this one: maybe men win at work because... they are just better? I'm sure there are people out there who secretly (and not always secretly) think this and that maybe we women should just accept it and let men do what they're best at.

Er, no, I don't think so.

There is *no* competence or intelligence gap between men and women. Men are not better. Women are not better. We can't move forwards if there are any question marks on this one, so in case anyone is not 100% convinced about this, let's look at the data.

Let's start with the fact that more than half of university students worldwide are women, including at the most prestigious institutions of higher education such as Harvard, Yale and Princeton.[1] Fifty-seven per cent of students in college or higher education in the US are women,[2] 55% in Europe.[3] Women earn 60% of all university degrees in the US, 30% of American women hold a bachelor's degree versus 28% of men.[4] In the US, women take more advanced placement

(AP) and honours classes in high school than men do; 61% of English Scholastic Assessment Test (SAT) takers were female versus 39% male. And just in case you're thinking that this is because girls and women are only taking on the arts and languages subjects, think again: 54% of Maths SAT takers were female versus 46% male, 54% of girls took 4 years of maths compared with 48% of boys, 55% of girls took algebra and geometry compared with 45% of boys and 56% of girls took other maths courses compared with 44% of boys.[5]

Whichever way you look at education data, you will see the same story – girls and women at least match boys and men in intelligence and academic performance, to the point that it is a long time since I have actually heard, or heard of, a man seriously question that women are men's equals in the brain department.

What many still question, however, is whether women's all-round skillset, including their leadership ability, is as strong as men's and whether they are therefore 'as good' for the big jobs versus being the 'Dependable Back-Up'.[6] The data says that they absolutely are. In 2009, *USA Today* compared the performance of the women CEOs of Fortune 500 companies (all 13 of them...) versus the performance of the men CEOs: the women CEOs' stocks were up 50% versus the average of 25%.[7] *Forbes* found that of the 26 publicly traded companies on its '2010 Power Women 100' list, those headed by women outperformed their industries by 15% and the overall market by 28%.[8]

A McKinsey report found that 89 European companies with the highest proportion of female leaders outperformed industry averages for the Stoxx Europe 600 with 10% higher return on equity, 48% higher earnings and 17 percentage points higher stock price growth.[9] Venture capital firm First Round reported that its investments in female-founded companies performed 63% better than those in all-male venture teams[10] and studies of hedge-fund managers showed that the women's funds outperformed the men's (I'll ask you to remember this later when we talk about men and women's attitude to risk).

Research done by a leadership development and training firm who surveyed 7,000 leaders showed that women outperformed men on 12 out of 16 measures of outstanding leadership (and scored the same on the other four).[11] Jack Zenger and Joseph Folkman's research, published in the *Harvard Business Review*, found that

> women are perceived by their managers – particularly their male managers – to be slightly more effective than men at every hierarchical level and in virtually every functional area of the organisation… excelling in taking initiative, acting with resilience, practising self-development, driving for results and displaying high integrity and honesty. In fact, they were thought to be more effective in 84% of the competencies… [12]

The GALLUP® 'Women in America' report also found that:

> Engagement is the most important factor for empowering individuals, teams and organisations to perform with excellence… the more engaged a team is, the more it delivers on business outcomes such as profitability and productivity.

And that:

> As employees and managers, women are more engaged at work than men are. Female managers also lead teams that are more engaged than male managers' teams. Clearly, women have the engagement edge.[13]

They saw that employees who work for a female manager are 6% more engaged, on average, than those who work for a male manager. Female employees who work for a female manager are the most engaged, male employees who report to a male manager are the least engaged. Employees who work for female managers give higher ratings to nearly all of GALLUP®'s employee engagement survey items than do employees who work for male managers. In summary they say:

> This finding suggests that female managers surpass their male counterparts in cultivating potential in others.[14]

As an aside, they also saw that only slightly more than a third of women are engaged at work – for all of the reasons we will discuss. Just imagine what organisations could achieve if we could engage more women!

Economist Esther Duflo of the Massachusetts Institute of Technology (MIT) found that women are more effective than men at running the village councils in India because they take fewer bribes and focus more resources on critical infrastructure.[15] Yang Mianmian of the Qingdao Refrigerator General Factory, named one of the 100 Most Powerful Women in the world by *Forbes* magazine from 2006 to 2008, says there is 'some bias' against women that she was able to overcome by 'setting a higher standard than the normal work standard.'[16]

Tomas Chamorro-Premuzic is clear on his view that women are the superior sex in his controversially titled book *Why Do So Many Incompetent Men Become Leaders?*:

> Women are better leaders. I am not neutral on this. I am sexist in favour of women. Women have better people skills, are more altruistic… They outperform men in university at graduate and undergraduate levels.[17]

Some do believe that women are generally better leaders than men, some that the women who make it to leadership positions had to be stronger than their male peers because of the gender barriers they have needed to overcome to get there: Sylvie Moreau of Coty told me she believes women need to be three times as good and three times as confident because she has to work three times harder to be heard! During the Covid-19 pandemic, it has become rather popular to suggest that the female country leaders have been stronger than the men. The suggestion has been that the women heads of state such as Angela Merkel of Germany, Jacinda Ardern and others have done a better job of handling the crisis based on listening to the experts, clear decision-making, swift response and consistent direction. By way of contrast, some of the male leaders have been accused of taking a macho, over-confident approach and making poor decisions as a consequence, resulting in lack of clarity and consistency. Now much as I have appreciated seeing so many role models of female leadership in the media (which can only be a positive thing), I do challenge this huge over-simplification of leadership and gender. What these women have in common, apart from being women, is that they are strong leaders but their leadership styles are very different: Merkel's approach is not like Ardern's, who's style is more like Canadian Justin Trudeau's. Some leadership approaches are for sure more effective than others, but what Kristof Neirynck, CMO (Chief Marketing Officer) of Global Brands at Walgreens Boots Alliance, calls 'the leadership style of the future', does not exclusively belong to women and all male leaders should not be judged because a couple of prominent ones made an embarrassing mess of managing this crisis. It is also, I believe, rather premature to claim victory for any leader before we see the long-term repercussions of Covid-19 on economies and mental health. So, for me the 'women are better leaders than men' argument is not helpful. Helen Lewis put it best in her article 'The Pandemic Has Revealed the Weakness of Strongmen':

> So, let's not flip the old sexist script. After centuries
> of dogma that men are naturally better suited to
> leadership, the opposite is not suddenly true.[18]

I think it's time for us to end the gender war and stop

debating which gender is superior – it puts aggressive, defensive barriers up between men and women and this is the last thing we need if we are going to move forward on this together.

For me this is simple – women and men may be different but they are equals and, most importantly, there is no intelligence or competence gap between them. So, the question remains, if women and men really are equal in ability, why do so few women get the c-suite jobs? Why are we not at 50/50 for men and women in all the senior roles? If men are not better than women, why are they still more successful? Why do they win at work?

Are you ready for the answer to this question, for the brutal reality? It is ultimately very simple. Men win at work because the people who promote them believe that they are better than the women. Men get most of the best jobs and hold a higher share of leadership positions because they are promoted more frequently than women – not because the people who make the decision are on a deliberate crusade to push men onwards and upwards and hold women down but because they truly believe that the men are better and will therefore perform better in the role.

I will never forget a discussion I had about gender diversity at my previous company with a group of people, men and women, that I like and respect very much. We were talking about the usual issue: why is it that we recruit 50% women but at each level we become slightly more male-biased until the jump from Manager level to Associate Director level when the percentage of women drops significantly. Now bear in mind that this group of people were voluntarily part of a team that was working on the gender issue, so they cared about it and wanted to work on addressing it. This was a very well-intentioned group. At one point we made the issue specific to try to penetrate it by discussing a recent promotion of a man by one of the men in the group (this man happened to be an absolute gentleman and one of the people I most admired in the company). I asked him to tell us why, ultimately, he had chosen the man for the role from all the options he had. His response was, 'I looked objectively at all the candidates and the man was the best.'

This reveals so much. This good man, this well-intentioned man who was in no way what anyone would describe as 'sexist', had done his due diligence, reviewed all his candidates 'fairly' and could therefore feel very comfortable with his conclusion that 'the man was the best'. Now, of course it is possible (around 50% possible you could say) that, in this specific instance, the man truly was the strongest and best person for the role. But what happened here is happening every day, in every company, in every organisation and the reality is that most of the time (90% plus of CEO appointment decisions, 80% plus of board position decisions, and so on…) the same conclusion is drawn – that the man is the best. Now that simply cannot be right.

One deep underlying issue here is 'the mini-me syndrome'. Psychologically, humans are primed to favour people who seem to be like them and therefore people tend to recruit and promote people who feel the 'same as me'. This 'cloning' is a natural phenomenon and one that starts early. Harvard social psychologist Mahzarin Banaji found that our preferences begin forming at the age of six and children will choose to be with other children who look similar to them.[19] Too often, we are still doing the same as adults when making hiring decisions where 'like is comfortable with like'.[20] The problem is it does not necessarily lead us to make good recruitment and appointment decisions if, 'The hiring manager hires for familiarity ahead of hiring for qualification,' as one CEO told me. And it goes beyond affecting our hiring decisions, it also affects how well we manage and grow the people who work for us. We all know that feedback helps people to develop but Professor Linda Hill of Harvard Business School found that people are more comfortable giving feedback to someone who is like them.[21] So even if we have resisted recruiting our mini-me, we may subconsciously not be helping our other employee to grow, either way, the self-fulfilling prophecy keeps on rolling.

Most of us are not aware that we are under the influence of all this, all we know is that we like the person, we feel good with them, we seem to be on the same wavelength about things and it feels good to work with them. So this means that what you have at the top usually cascades down as people bring in and promote their mini-mes and, given that men hold most of the senior positions in our society, if they keep cloning themselves with mini-mes then women are going to really struggle to get a look in. And this mini-me syndrome is not just an issue for women, it is an issue for the whole team and their performance – anyone who knows anything about building high performing teams will tell you that homogeneity of thought is the enemy of innovation and that promoting and developing your mini-me is not the best choice. Another one of you is exactly what you don't need on your team. You need someone who sees things differently and sees the things you would otherwise miss. You need diversity.

So, the brutal and simple reality – men think men are better and stronger performers and men currently have most of the senior positions and promotions, and role allocations are decisions mostly made by men. So, it follows that men get these promotions and roles over women. Thus, the self-fulfilling prophecy of male domination at the senior levels continues – and this will keep on fulfilling itself until the end of time if we don't consciously intervene.

5

The invisible power of culture
(and other forces)

LET'S NOW TALK about why people believe that men are better than women (and thus more often than not land the big job or the promotion), when we know from all of the data that they are not. One of the key reasons is the invisible power of workplace culture, which is created when there are dominant and non-dominant groups, and is intangible and unconscious for most. I love the metaphor from Men Advocating Real Change (MARC), who talk of training a goldfish in the water – if you ask him how the water is, he will be rather puzzled and ask you, 'Er, what water…?'[1] A dominant culture is only really noticed by those that are foreign to it.

Let's consider the invisible power of culture from a race point of view. White people don't have to think about their race, whereas BAME people will tell you that they constantly do. Holidaying with one of my greatest friends has taught me this. She is of Indian origin and I have seen her treated differently from me on a number of occasions. One of the worst examples was at a famous hotel in Miami. I locked myself out of our room one day and went to the reception desk to ask for a new key, which I received with no trouble. Two days later, my friend lost her key and went to the same receptionist with the same request, only this time she faced a barrage of questions and an ID check before she got her replacement key.

And that's not all. On our last night of the holiday, we

returned to the hotel and there was a security guy on the door (they had a fancy event that night). I was allowed to enter the hotel without incident but my friend, right behind me, was stopped and questioned. There was only one difference between us and that is the colour of our skin. Suffice to say we won't be going back to that hotel...

This has given me a very small insight into the scale of privilege I have as a white person, but the reality is that white people are part of a dominant culture that they are mostly unaware of. Similarly, when men are operating in a dominant male culture, of course many of them don't notice it and are not aware that it is sometimes uncomfortable and difficult for the women who are trying to operate in it. One man was genuinely puzzled when I shared with him the things women experience in a male environment (for example, being talked over in a meeting). He told me that he had never witnessed these things and did not recognise them at all. Of course not – he's a man!

I witnessed one jaw-dropping example of this blindness to the dominant culture. A group of senior leaders had spent two days out of the office on gender diversity training that had done a good job of opening up awareness of how women experienced things versus men. One of the biggest discussions had been around executive board meetings, which were male-dominated (in line with the high percentage of men at the senior level seen at most companies) and not seen as very constructive or fruitful by the women on the team (more on the pain of male-dominated meetings later). After hours of discussion on this and the negative experiences of the women on the team, one of the male leaders demonstrated the difficulty of seeing a culture that you are part of and comfortable in. With a small introductory cough, he said, 'Well I personally have to say that I really like and enjoy these meetings.' The point had clearly gone completely over his head and I think my jaw may have actually dropped open. I would have found it funny if I had not been so distressed that we had all wasted so much time discussing something that was clearly completely lost on most of these men: the male-dominant culture was invisible to them.

Even I as a woman didn't notice the dominant male culture at work for many years – probably because before I was at Director level I was working on teams and participating in meetings that were close to 50/50 male/female. I recognise, by the way, that I was lucky in this, which was partly a result of my marketing role (which is generally one that attracts more women) and partly a result of the fact that my company was one of the better ones when it came to gender equality and diversity and put a lot of focus on it. I am very aware that my female colleagues in sales or product supply and my friends in other companies hit the dominant male culture much earlier in their careers. I personally hit it later when I was promoted to Vice-President level.

It is, thankfully, pretty rare in this day and age, at least in a self-respecting company or organisation, for men to consciously leverage their dominant position in their team and culture against women to make them look and feel small and to weaken them. Let's not ignore that it does happen though. One of my great friends told me a story from when she was working with an entirely male team at a well-known retailer. She was consistently struggling to make herself heard in meetings until one day one of the men raised his hand to the group and said, 'Shush, the little lady is trying to speak.' I'm sure you can imagine how comfortable, valued and empowered my friend felt after that – which is, I'm sure exactly, what he wanted (in what Laura Bates describes as 'an exertion of power, dominance and control').[2] It even happens in the House of Commons. In 2013, Caroline Lucas MP, raised concerns over media sexism and the then Prime Minister David Cameron and the men on his front bench laughed at her.[3] At its worst, a male-dominant culture can turn the men into bullies of their isolated, weakened female victims.

These are awful examples, but they are the extreme and there is little doubt that most of the men in a male-dominant culture are not at all conscious of belonging to it most, if not all, of the time. 'Privilege is invisible to those who have it', as Dr Michael Kimmel says.[4] The man in the male-dominant culture is like the goldfish, he takes his environment for granted and he is not even aware it is there, but of course it is very visible and tangible to others.

If the culture of a company is white, male, Anglo-Saxon, and you are all of these things, congratulations, you are a goldfish and you are going to feel very at home in the company water. But if you are not all of these things, or especially if you are not any of these things, you are not going to feel at home at all. It is hard to be in the goldfish water if you're not a goldfish – and the further away from being a goldfish you are, the harder it gets. In Laura Liswood's words, 'We walk in different worlds based on who we are.'[5] Importantly, dealing with the 'male kingdom' (in the words of Dina Dublin, ex-CFO of JPMorgan Chase) is so difficult because it is subconscious rather than blatant and deliberately unfair. As she says, 'It is narrow-minded and ineffective, but human.'[6]

So why is it so hard to exist in a culture that isn't your own? Why is this issue important if you are a woman in a dominant male culture?

First, in any situation, the dominant group always benefits from presumed competence, while the non-dominant group's competence is questioned, or at least needs to be demonstrated and proven. This means the non-dominant group needs to navigate the culture in a different way and work harder to prove themselves.

This is true even at the highest levels. Laura Liswood has interviewed every female President and Prime Minister in history and across the globe, and concluded that

Most of the world's women leaders said they were treated differently from their male colleagues.

She describes her personal experience of how this feels:

> Throughout my career in business, I have often felt
> what I call disappeared… We just weren't being seen
> or heard in the same way that men were. Our impact
> and presence seemed muted in comparison.

It's another downward spiral where

> diverse people get discouraged, perceive themselves as
> less valued, reduce confidence in themselves.[7]

In fact, it is proven that women actually *do* perform less well
in male presence. This starts with the issue that it is 'his game
not my game' or, as Dr Kimmel puts it, as if men are saying,
'You are welcome to join us, but we're not going to change
the menu.'[8] We all perform better when we play a game that
we invented or at least where we are in control and know how
it is played. The problem runs much deeper than this though.
The theory goes that when we are in our 'own culture', we
feel a natural state of inclusion. Nobody has to remember to
include us in things, we are just part of it. This is a good feeling;
we feel calm and comfortable – we have a sense of belonging in
this environment without having to moderate what we do or
say, or try to copy others in order to 'fit in'. As a result, we feel
relaxed and confident, we can perform at our best. Of course,
this means that the opposite scenario can also be true, and
feelings of exclusion can occur just as easily, meaning we are
not relaxed, we are not confident and so we can't perform at
our best. If our style does not match the preferred style, we do
not feel confident and relaxed and as a result we do not seem
confident. This impacts how comfortable people feel with us
and, as Heather Wilson, US Representative of New Mexico
rightly says, 'part of being a good public leader is having
people comfortable with you.'[9] Interestingly, research also
shows that a feeling of belonging is a more major concern

for women in general – and so being in a culture that is not 'theirs', which of course they so often are, has a bigger impact on them and their degree of comfort and confidence than it would a man. We should say at this point, however, that it is not only women who feel a lack of belonging in a male-dominant culture – many men can feel it too. I am sure that one of the dynamics here is that women overestimate how comfortable everybody else is feeling and underestimate how much others may be trying to appear to be fitting in. Perhaps if we were all aware that we are not the only ones who do not feel like we 'belong', we would paradoxically feel more comfortable and like we therefore, well, belong.

What is very important here is that, in a male-dominant culture, all of this lack of comfort and belonging is invisible to most of the men who feel at ease in the culture. Also, by the way, some women may also not be conscious of it either because they are used to the feeling of not fully belonging. A financial institution did an internal study of four groups: white American men, white American women, American minorities and non-Americans and found that:

> One of the groups thought the organisation was
> a meritocracy… It didn't necessarily make the
> dominant group uncaring… they merely assumed
> their experiences were the same as others… They were
> confident that hard work pays off, and that the salary
> and promotions were handed out fairly and justly.[10]

The white American men were the only group to experience the culture this way because it is extremely difficult for members of dominant groups to put themselves into the shoes (or even be aware of the shoes) of the members of non-dominant groups. The lack of inclusion, belonging and comfort of the non-dominant groups is not tangible – all that can be seen is the end result, of it, which is the person's authenticity and performance. 'He's just stronger' is what's felt, and not the reasons underneath.

Critically, it is not just a person's performance that is affected by their degree of comfort in the culture, it is also how authentic they seem to be to others – and this is fundamental. When we don't feel inclusion, we don't feel a sense of belonging, and the need to belong is so fundamental in us all that we try to 'fit in' in order to feel it. Sarah Cooper knows this – she hilariously includes a set of wearable moustaches in her book to allow women to seem more man-like. But, even without the wearable moustache, when we try to fit in with the men, we are not being our authentic self. And this unsettles others – people can't put their finger on it, but they sense there is something not quite right, something people don't trust. Authenticity is something that people can read from our face and body language and, by definition, it is difficult to 'do authenticity' – as Jean-Paul Sartre noted, to try to be authentic is to fail.[11] So the only way to be authentic is to actually *be authentic*. But we can't look or feel authentic if we are not feeling relaxed, comfortable, at home, 'ourselves'. This is one of the biggest disadvantages for women in a male culture – the men feel they belong and so can be and feel authentic, the women don't and therefore can't.

Margaret Thatcher was famous for being a woman who adapted her style to fit in. She succeeded with her male-dominant group (more on her later), but this has not proved to be a role model approach that other women have successfully followed. One of the most interesting examples we have seen of this was the 2016 presidential election campaign of Hillary Clinton. Jennifer Palmieri, Communications adviser to Clinton and author of *Dear Madam President*, shared some fascinating insights in her talk at the Royal Society of Arts in London. For her, the key mistake Clinton's campaign made was turning Clinton into a 'female facsimile of a male leader, mimicking male qualities'. By definition, she was 'copying' and, as a result, people found her inauthentic. The feedback they consistently heard (and, let's face it, many of us heard it – some of us probably even said it) was, 'There's something about her I just don't like and I just don't trust.'[12] In the absence of any role model for a female US President, she tried to fit in with the male ones and look like she belonged in the world that had hitherto been dominated by men.

We all know how badly this backfired for her (and, one could argue, for the US and rest of world). It is easy to ask why she did not just show up as her authentic self so people could trust her. If you are a man, who looks and acts like all the men who have gone before you in a job, if you are a goldfish and the water feels very comfortable to you, it is the most natural thing in the world to just be yourself. Anyone who has been in an alien culture, with no role models to reassure them, knows that it is extremely difficult to find the strength and courage to bring your very different, authentic self to the game. We fear that we will not fit in and won't be accepted. For me, one of the most interesting qualities about Hillary Clinton is that she's a very honest and direct woman, according to Jennifer Palmieri – that's why she was so truly terrible at 'faking it'. How ironic it is that a dishonest person would find it easier to fake male leadership qualities and would seem more authentic and trustworthy. Consider how costly all this is when it leads to the wrong decision being made.

Not all roles are like that of the President of the US, but the male-dominant culture impacts women everywhere, how they perform and how they are perceived. A great friend of mine was struggling to get to manager level at her company. Every year she was hitting and exceeding her targets but, when it was time for her annual review, she was told she wasn't quite ready for promotion yet. Nobody could tell her the reason for this, there was just an intangible sense from her managers that 'something was missing'. She felt lost – she wasn't comfortable in her current role and didn't really enjoy it, but she had been persevering because she wanted the promotion to manager that had been her goal. I asked her to imagine the promotion was off the table. What would she like to do? It turned out that there was another new department in her company that she would love to work in. I asked her if she thought she would be happier in that job at her current level or promoted in the department she was working in at the time. She was very clear that the answer was the new department. So, when she returned to work after a vacation, she gathered her courage and told her bosses that she wanted to leave the current team and transfer to the new department and do work that she would enjoy in an environment that felt right for her. They told her that she would miss out on promotion and she said, 'So be it, this is more important.' And guess what? A few months later, she got her promotion after all. But it didn't stop there. At her next annual review, her new manager started talking about promotion to the next level of Director, with a view to being on the path for potential partner in the future.

What happened here is that she discovered what she wanted, and needed, and got herself out of a place and role she didn't belong in and into one where she did. As a result, she felt comfortable, relaxed and able to be her authentic self. Everyone around her could feel this and suddenly stopped thinking there was something missing and started thinking she was absolutely brilliant and should be promoted and re-promoted. And she was. She was the same woman as the one who had been struggling to be recognised, valued and rewarded just a couple of years before, but when she was in a different environment and culture (which was also less male-dominated by the way) she was able to be more herself.

But not every woman is lucky enough to get herself out and where she should be. As a result, we are all missing out on this unfulfilled female potential. It is so important that we are aware of the negative effect that a male-dominant culture has on the women who don't belong in it – how they perform, how we perceive them, the confidence we have in them and, as a result, on the decisions we make about their ability (or not) to perform in a job versus the other options for the role. Catalyst research has found that:

Women who felt like an 'other' based on one or more characteristics were less likely to be in positions of power and received fewer promotions.[13]

And also, positively, that when people feel valued for being unique, they deliver more innovation.

The invisible power of culture, belonging and authenticity is at play for women everywhere – in the male-dominant culture of our organisations and businesses we may be equal, but we are not the same. Not being the same leads to invisible and intangible behaviours that lead to the perception that women are not equal in intelligence and competence. In fact, some argue that women who even begin to compete and perform in male-dominant culture are not just equal but must be even stronger than men in order to overcome the odds stacked against them. Writer John Scalzi puts this absolutely brilliantly:

In the role playing game known as The Real World, 'Straight White Male' is the lowest difficulty setting there is.[14]

It is quite ironic in fact that men generally love to compete and be seen to compete at the highest level and standard possible and yet they are content to play on the lowest difficulty setting at work.

And culture is not the only invisible force working against women; unconscious bias is another invisible monster that lies very deep in us all. Cognitive bias is simply what the brain does in order to maximise its efficiency when faced with an overwhelming number of inputs from every direction every day. As Joshua Burkhart says of the brain in his article, 'We're Half Blind Until We Work With the Unconscious':

It likes information it is familiar with, it selects it and includes it, neuron linked to neuron, to consolidate its worldview... always trying to maximise efficiency and conserve resources, the brain doesn't like to rewire its neurons.[15]

As a result, the brain will naturally default to categorising things in the easiest, most obvious place in keeping with where it has learnt over time that those things belong. This means that there are some fundamental assumptions about women that, like all stereotypes, are difficult to shake off, for men and for women. At an unconscious level, women can be seen as either sex objects or mothers, as either pretty or clever, as either strong or likeable . One of my favourite stories is from my gorgeous, blonde and highly intelligent friend Olesya Nazarova, founder and CEO of APPAREAL™. She entered a national Physics competition when she was young but when she arrived, was told by the organiser, 'Little chicken, you are in the wrong place.' She felt completely discouraged and started to doubt herself, questioning what she was doing there and whether she should just walk out and run away. But she didn't – she pulled herself together, decided not to let this man affect her, and stayed and won the prize. The brilliant consultant Susan Van Vleet believed that the reason I wasn't valued as highly by my management as my male peers was 'you look more like their wife than their colleague and they don't know what to do with that'. This aligns with Carol Tarvis and Elliot Aronson's 'implicit theory', which states that once people have a bias the confirmation bias kicks in and they stop seeing evidence that doesn't fit their theory and give too much weight to evidence that does.[16]

We all have unconscious bias towards some things, 80% of the mind works unconsciously.[17] Biases do not come from bad intentions and nobody is immune from them. I love the famous example of the top five orchestras in the US. In 1970, they were made up of only 5% women, so they started blind auditions (the Boston Symphony Orchestra was the first) and made progress to 35%.[18] But at first the blind auditions didn't work to shift the gender balance – it only started working when they asked the auditionees to remove their shoes before they walked onto the stage – because the panel could hear the women's heels.

The issue is that we all involuntarily bring our subconscious selves and subconscious beliefs about others into the workplace. Subtle advantages are continuously given to those who match our expectation of a strong performer or leader. As one senior female TV presenter told me about personnel decisions she has seen: 'It's not intended to be bias; it just can't see past the old model of itself.'

And it isn't just men who are subconsciously biased against women, women can also be subconsciously sexist to other women. A study by scientists at Yale University looked at app-lications sent to universities for science-based jobs. The CVs were identical except some had male names and some female – recruiters, both male and female, rated the male applicants as 'significantly more competent and hireable' and also offered the male applicants a higher starting salary.[19]

GALLUP® found that Americans are more likely to say they would prefer a male boss (33%) to a female boss (20%), with women also more likely to say they would prefer a male boss (despite women often being better at managing people than men are).[20] In one study in the venture capital world involving an audio-based pitch competition, the same narrative was read out by a man and a woman and 60% of the audience backed the venture pitched by the man.[21]

Closer to home, a very good friend of mine once admitted to me (with some clear embarrassment) that if her son needed important and risky surgery, she would be more comfortable with a male doctor doing it. This from a highly intelligent and successful woman! So, if even she feels this way then it's a good indication that gender bias against women is pretty much everywhere. I enjoyed the slant put on this in *Ocean's 8*, when Sandra Bullock's character Debbie Ocean explains why she doesn't want a 'him' on the team she is putting together to steal some diamonds: 'A him gets noticed and a her gets ignored – and for once we want to be ignored.' Amusing in a film, not so much for women in life and at work. Some would say that the biggest thing we are fighting is not in fact a gender diversity issue but a bias issue – that the problem is that the subconscious handling of our bias in the face of diversity creates the lack of fairness towards women.

We can tell ourselves that these subconscious ways that men see women are just general stereotypes, not important and not relevant to how a specific woman is perceived or treated at work. My concern, however, is that underneath it all, even the men who know to avoid saying and doing inappropriate, sexist things have, under the surface, a subconscious but still pretty low opinion of women (beyond being sexual partners, wives and mothers) – and that, in some form, this comes out as anything from not listening properly to women in meetings to influencing job and promotion decisions. My fear is shared by Laura Bates who believes that this

> assumption of female inferiority often translates into
> a similarly casual assumption of women's professional
> inferiority.[22]

If we are not conscious of the way that the unconscious is negatively affecting our view of the world – and specifically of women – our view will have many blind spots and, worse, be based on false perceptions. Or, as psychoanalyst Carl Jung put it, 'Until you make the unconscious conscious, it will direct your life'.[23]

Marilyn Monroe is quoted as saying, 'I do not mind living in a man's world as long as I can be a woman in it'.[24] This may be very cute but, once we understand the invisible power of the male-dominant culture then we have to say, 'Well Marilyn, I do mind!' Because we can't live in a man's world and truly be women in it, we can't live in a male-dominant culture and be our authentic selves, and we can't live in a man's world with all of its unconscious bias against us, at least not if we want to have a successful career and do justice to our potential. To leverage the brains and the capability of women, we have to create a culture that we can feel we belong in too – not a male-dominant culture, not a man's world, but a shared world.

6

The science bit

DO YOU REMEMBER my warning at the beginning about needing to make generalisations about men versus women in order to talk about this issue? Well I'm afraid the generalisations are going to really kick in now and some of you aren't going to like it. Please bear with me though. If you don't believe some of this is true for you and you don't associate yourselves with some of these science-based hypotheses and conclusions, nobody is forcing it upon you personally – but please be aware that they *are* true for many people.

So, it's time for the science bit.

We have seen that one of the reasons that men are more successful at work is because they fit, belong and therefore perform, and are perceived to perform, better in the established male-dominant culture. But is that all there is to it? Many believe not and that it is not just our male-female biology but also our ancestry that has played an important part in our development and how we behave today.

Now I'm no scientist but there is a lot of research and evidence to support the idea that boys and girls just aren't made the same way from the start, including from University of Cambridge neuroscientist Professor Simon Baron Cohen's experiment with 100 babies. One-day-old babies were shown two objects and the boys clearly responded more to the mechanical object and the girls to the human face.[1] Louann Brizendine's case on the science-based differences between women and men in *The Female Brain* is controversial and not universally supported, I know, but I personally find it interesting and worth sharing nonetheless. Brizendine lays out many differences between the male and the female brain that affect the way we react and behave, including at work. She tells us that the amygdalae is the brain's fear centre and that FMRI scans show that women activate theirs more easily in response to negative events. The psychological stress of conflict resonates more deeply in the female brain, creating a sudden change in serotonin and dopamine which causes a kind of mini brain seizure. (Not surprisingly, women would generally prefer to avoid having a mini brain seizure if they possibly can and therefore tend to try to avoid stressful conflicts.) In addition, the anterior cingulate cortex, known as the 'worry wort centre', that weighs options and makes decisions is larger in women.[2] The hippocampus, which is the principle hub of emotion formation and observation, is also larger in women. Therefore, there is a basis in science for women generally being more sensitive or easily offended than men and more prone to feel and therefore show strong emotions (I lost count long ago of how many women I have heard be discounted by a man as 'too emotional'). Meanwhile, men have twice as many serotonin receptors as women, so women need double the external feedback and boosting to stimulate it. Their happiness and motivation levels are more affected if there is a lack of that. Oestrogen, the main female hormonal driver, encourages bonding, connection, sensitivity and collaboration, and creates a strong aversion to conflict and risk-taking. Testosterone, on the other hand, is the main male hormonal driver (men have ten times more of it than women do) which affects speed, strength, muscle size, competitive instinct and aggression, and encourages hierarchy and the demonstration of risk-taking and power.[3]

A small pause here on the 'risk-taking' point as I'm sure many of you will be raising your eyebrows. Risk-taking is a good thing and people who are comfortable with taking risks are really cool, impressive and the best performers, right? I'm sure many women won't like to be seen as less willing to take risks. And many men will be quietly thinking to themselves, 'Yeah, that's the problem with women – they're very solid and reliable but they don't like taking risks, so they don't deliver breakthrough results.' One of my brilliant female friends, for example, was told early in her career by the Director that although he rated her 'excellent', she 'would never hit one out of the ballpark'.

However, sexy as risk-taking seems, let's remember that a 'testosterone-laced decision isn't always a better one'.[4] It may feel and look exciting and macho at the time, but I would ask you to remember those male leaders who went into aggressive, warrior mode and were impulsive in their management of the Covid-19 crisis, or those successful female hedge-fund managers we talked about in 'Do you have feminist phobia?'. Financial trader John Coates found that traders' profits drove male testosterone up, leading to them taking more risks – and ultimately too many.[5] Research into 3,600 companies found that female executives perform better than men on M&A (merger and acquisition) deals, indicating they are more meticulous in investment decision-making. We need to be aware of the dangers of testosterone and not fall into the trap of admiring the risk-taker; we always need to be conscious of responding to people and behaviours positively without looking at the facts and their results.

Testosterone is also shown to improve your confidence which, in turn, causes other people to see you as more positive and trustworthy. We'll talk more about the huge importance of projecting confidence in the next chapter. It's a key driver of men's success and, what's more, the testosterone/confidence link is a positive spiral – positive, confident body language increases testosterone levels by 20% and reduces cortisol levels by 25%. As reducing cortisol minimises stress and enables you to think more clearly in difficult and challenging situations, so people with high testosterone and low cortisol are shown to be people who thrive under pressure.[6]

As self-professed 'neurobiology geek' Dr Stephanie Estima says, 'Our biology hasn't changed much in 10,000 years'.[7] And this is working in many ways against women as they try to compete with their natural biology in the business and working world, where the classic 'male' testosterone-driven traits are more associated with leadership and success. There is also a view that, beyond our biology, women and men have evolved and developed differently based on the roles we played in early society. While the men went out hunting for food, the women stayed in the community to care for the children: each gender had to develop different skills to succeed in their role. For the women it was critical to stay on the right side of and not alienate the other women in their community, so they were socialised as peacekeepers and learnt the importance of collaboration, smooth communication and not trying to be, or appearing to be, above anyone else. We see in the way many women communicate with each other today how they neutralise a compliment they are given to ensure they are not perceived as immodest or too big for their boots. And equally we see how women react to another woman who does allow herself to be set up and perceived as 'superior' to others in some way – she will be disliked and, ultimately, excluded if she doesn't quickly find some humility.

All of this starts when women are still girls. There is a wonderful example of this in the way seven-year-olds behaved when they were put into teams and observed – one team of boys, one team of girls.[8] Each team was allocated a captain. The boys' captain was very comfortable to take on the responsibility of the role and the command, and the other boys were totally happy to accept that he was the 'boss' and to follow his lead (while no doubt secretly hoping that one day, they would get to be captain themselves). Meanwhile it was a very different dynamic in the girls' team, where the captain quickly established that they were a team and they would make plans and decisions together, listening to and taking on board everyone's point of view. We see here how boys accept other boys being 'above' them and, when the time comes, they accept the responsibility of being the captain themselves. Girls, however, demonstrate more need for 'levelling' – I'm not above you, you're not above me, we're equal. This sticks over time – power is often embarrassing for women to accept, both in themselves and in other women. They can be less comfortable than men in giving orders or positioning themselves (or being positioned) above other women.

Let's think about all this socialisation in the context of work. We have the females, programmed since the beginning of time to keep themselves 'on the same level' as the other females, not allowing themselves to be seen as thinking they are 'superior', even when put in a position of authority, always looking for a way to ensure everyone feels 'equal'. And then we have the males, the hunters, they love to be 'top dog' but are happy to accept whoever is in power and to accept their authority. They feel naturally more comfortable in a working environment where taking on a position of responsibility is highly valued and they must be perplexed when they see women communicating with female-relating techniques such as self-deprecation to keep everyone on an equal level; ensuring everyone is included; constantly saying 'I'm sorry'; and gendered speech patterns with open-ended rather than direct, definitive statements such as 'We might want to consider', so as not to 'bulldoze' and appear too forceful or closed. These are all techniques easily recognised by other women but often seen as rambling, inconclusive and weak by men.

There is one more deep evolutionary dynamic at play between men and women and it almost certainly always will be. It is an undeniable truth that men, on average, are physically stronger than women. (Yes, there are some women who are stronger than some men, but the strongest man on the planet will always be stronger than the strongest woman.) Every man knows this, every woman knows this, and the result is that, at a deep and usually subconscious level, many women are afraid of men. There is a brilliant quote from

Margaret Atwood from the 1980s that:

> Men are afraid that women will laugh at them.
> Women are afraid that men will kill them.[9]

And while it seems extreme to say this in the context of men and women at work, it is an important dynamic. It is not, of course, that a woman believes that the man across the table from her in the meeting is going to kill or physically hurt her, but she may be carrying with her years of experience, perhaps from childhood, of the threat of male physical power and dominance over her. If she is lucky, this has not been used against her, either as intimidation or an actual violent act, but it has created psychological memories that influence her, which are quietly and invisibly present every time she interacts with a man. Women may not realise it at the time, but these experiences and memories of male physical dominance have an impact on how they interact with and communicate with men. This is eloquently expressed in Sarah Vaughan's *Anatomy of a Scandal*:

> women are often scared of antagonising their
> assailants… we women aim to please. It is hardwired
> into us that we should placate and mollify, bend our
> will to that of men.[10]

I remember doing an exercise a few years ago on Susan Van Vleet's life-changing Women Moving Forward® course. She asked us all to recall three occasions of when we had been let down or harmed by a man and to write letters to each of these men. I spent a lot of time on writing mine and was rather pleased with them, but when I read them out to Susan and the group, she was unimpressed. She looked at me and said:

> Your homework for tonight is to re-write them, but
> this time without all the apologies, understanding and

explanations for what they did – I want you to unleash
your anger on them.

So, I went home that evening and tried again. But I cannot tell
you how difficult it was for me – it felt like being constipated,
like the words physically could not come out. When I told
Susan this the next day, her sage response was simply, 'I
wonder who taught you that you need to talk to men that
way.' She didn't need to say anything else and she didn't need
to know anything about my experience of men in my earlier
life. All she needed to know was that I was a woman and that
probably that meant that, at some point, I had probably been
physically hurt by a man or experienced the threat of this,
and that this could be what had taught me to be careful with
my words and not to push them too far. I have thought very
deeply about this, then and many times since. I am a woman
who is known for saying what I think openly and directly but
Susan made me realise that this is only true to a certain point.
There had been moments during my career, in meetings and
discussions with men, when I had pressed a point hard but
ultimately stopped and held back, careful not to push them
too far, not to make them angry. While I didn't realise this
consciously at the time, at a subliminal level this was fear –
fear of male anger, fear of male power, fear of men.

This is a personal example, but I know from many
other women that this resonates with them. So, why is this
dynamic important? Because if we, as women, are holding
back and backing off even slightly on the points we need to
make in a discussion or argument, if we are afraid to push an
important message that we need to deliver as far as it needs
to be pushed, even if that means us getting into an aggressive
or angry altercation with a man, then we are not performing
and contributing to 100% of our ability – and, importantly,
most of the men around us don't have this same fear and this
limitation. I also wonder if it goes deeper than this – do we all
unconsciously sense this underlying fear in women? Do we at

some level feel that a man will fight to the end because he is not afraid to, but a woman will, eventually, back off? Is this part of the reason why we generally find men more impressive than women?

What is for certain is that, in the competition that is work, the men have the advantage over the women who fear pushing them too far – and so men win again. In *The Power* by Naomi Alderman, she presents an allegory of how the world would be if women had the physical power and took control over men.[11] They become the ones who are afraid and at the mercy of female whim. It would be fascinating to see how this reversal would play in the workplace and impact men's willingness to push too hard – no doubt they would be perceived as the less impressive gender and be less successful as a result. Interesting as this is to ponder, it of course would not help us to simply switch the power from one gender to another. It is gender and power balance and equality we need to get to. As we strive for this, let's not underestimate the power of our biology, the power of the unconscious, perhaps of things we have inherited from our ancestors, possibly even designed into us and our minds at the very beginning of time. We need to be aware of them, because they are all playing an invisible and key role in helping women to lose and men to win at work.

7

The confidence vs competence equation

WE ALL RECOGNISE someone we think looks and talks like a leader. People who speak up as opposed to staying quiet look like leaders. People who speak up early look even more like leaders. People who speak at length versus make brief points look like leaders. So do people who are calm and relaxed; people who speak strongly and loudly; people who make bold statements, people who don't sound tentative or apologetic. People who assert certainty, versus suggesting they have shortcomings or doubts, who use strong, expansive body language. People who are tall are also more readily assumed to be leaders. The problem is that we find all of these attributes much more often in men than in women, for reasons that have nothing to do with their actual leadership ability.

One of the words we so often hear attributed to great leaders is 'gravitas', which in Latin means 'weight' or 'heaviness'.[1] So it literally means to speak with weight in your words. Ask yourself at this point if you ever heard a woman described as 'having gravitas' or have you ever described a woman that way yourself? A Duke University study showed a bias to lower voices[2] – and guess what gives a person a lower voice? Yes, testosterone, the male hormone. Many women in top leadership roles admit to having changed their communication style in order to be heard and Margaret Thatcher is a well-known example. She received feedback that her voice was too high and, like many women's voices, rose at the end of sentences, as if a question was being asked. (This is a female relational 'modesty' technique that women learn at a young age but that men hear as a lack of confidence in women.) In order to be taken more seriously as a leader, she learnt to speak in the way men speak, eliminating conditional words and the 'question inflection' at the end of sentences.[3] Laura Liswood witnessed the impact Thatcher has on men versus the impact of other leading women:

> When men watch my video documentary of my interviews with women Presidents and Prime Ministers, they typically lean forward, sit up straighter and listen closely when Thatcher is speaking.[4]

Thatcher was taken more seriously as a leader by men and is one of the exceptions who has managed to pull off 'faking' rather than being her authentic female self and not suffering for it (perhaps because, as one man said when he was asked why he admired her as a leader, 'she was basically a man anyway').[5] Theranos founder Elizabeth Holmes was arguably less successful than Thatcher with this strategy, with many former employees commenting unfavourably on her fake deep voice.

I was recently discussing all this with a female mathematics teacher. She told me that, while she has never been in business or politics, she completely recognises all of this from her career world. She shared how important oratory performance and depth of voice are in gaining and retaining authority in the classroom and that, as a result, male teachers are perceived to have more natural authority even if they are significantly younger and less experienced than the female teachers. She was happy to admit that she had learnt early on in her teaching career that she would need to 'perform' and use her 'deep voice' if she was going to have control over her students. So, we see these same issues affecting women across the board, whatever area they are working in, when they are required to convey leadership or authority (and isn't what we often see as leadership, in the end, an air of authority?).

What underlies many of the things that look like leadership and authority (talking loudly, boldly, and often with certainty) is a projection of confidence and self-assurance. People listen to and admire the most self-assured person, not necessarily the most knowledgeable or capable person.[6] And men seem to be forgiven when they have high confidence but little content, while even women with very strong competence and content can go unheard.

The confidence gap between women and men has been well documented, but why is it that women project less confidence? Importantly, they don't just *seem* to be less confident than men, they *are* actually less confident than men. Even Facebook COO (Chief Operations Officer) Sheryl Sandberg has said that, 'There are still days I wake up feeling like a fraud, not sure I should be where I am.'[7] Gerri Elliott, formerly of Juniper Networks, told a story about a presenter who asked a group of men and women if anyone had expertise in breast-feeding. Only a man raised his hand (based on having watched his wife do it), none of the mothers put themselves forward.[8]

Hewlett Packard (HP) research famously found that women only applied for a promotion if they believed they met 100% of the criteria for the role,[9] while the men had the confidence to apply if they met 60% upwards of the criteria and Laszlo Bock of Google saw that women were consistently less likely to nominate themselves for promotion.[10] Dr Richard Fox, Professor of Political Science at Loyola Marymount University, found that men are 65% more likely to view themselves as qualified to run for office.[11] Professor Marilyn Davidson of Manchester Business School carried out a study asking students what salary they deserve five years after graduation – the men said on average £52,000 and the women said £41,000.[12] Authors Linda Babcock and Sara Laschever found that women estimate fair pay as 4% less for first job than a comparable male salary, and 23% less at career peak.[13]

The evidence of men's higher degree of confidence is everywhere, with many studies showing that men overestimate their abilities and performance and women underestimate theirs. Psychologists conducted quiz-based research. Before the quiz each participant was asked to rate their scientific skills – the men rated themselves an average of 7.6 out of 10, the women 6.5. After the test, they were asked to rate themselves again and this time the men averaged 7.5 out of 10 and the women's rating dropped to a 5.8 average. In fact, the women's actual quiz results were just as good as the men's – another clear example of the gap between competence and confidence. This was reinforced when the participants were invited to enter a competition to win prizes – 71% of the men signed up but only 49% of the women, despite the fact that the women were just as capable.[14] In another experiment, groups had to select a leader to do a maths task after a five minute consultation together. In the discussion, the men were seen to overestimate their past performance by 30% plus and, as a result, were chosen to lead the group. This is yet more evidence that leaders are recognised and chosen more for their confidence than for their competence.

One driver of this problem is that men are more likely to have 'positive allusion' – they are likely to hear positives about themselves first, while women hear the opposite, the negatives. Linked to this, women's performance increases after positive feedback and decreases after negative feedback.[15] So if managers talk and give feedback to women as if they were men, this is going to further undermine confidence and do the opposite of helping them to succeed. Given how male-heavy management is, it is likely this is the case.

One of the most important signs of confidence is a degree of certainty and absence of doubt. When we sense doubt, we feel a lack of confidence from (and in) a person. This is a critical factor as we evaluate men versus women as leaders, or as potential leaders, because it is proven that women are more averse than men to uncertainty, guessing and risk-taking.

Research psychologist Zachary Estes gave 500 students tests with 3D images.[16] The women scored significantly worse but, thankfully, he was not someone who was ready to put this down to a competence gap between men and women. So, he analysed why it had happened. What he found was that the women hadn't attempted many of the questions because they didn't 'know' the answer. He ran the test again, but this time forced the participants to answer each question.

So why don't most women like to answer questions unless they are totally sure of the answer? It's known as atelophobia – the fear of imperfection, the fear of not being good enough or the 'curse of perfectionism'. Some women only feel confident when they know they are perfect and have a strong fear of failure. The famous article 'The Gifted Woman as Imposter' puts it well: 'women simply do not feel entitled to make mistakes. They… assume more ownership for mistakes.'[17]

I believe that discomfort with uncertainty and guessing is an absolutely critical differentiator between men and women. In that split second when a woman is put on the spot and asked a question, for example in a big meeting with her bosses, if she is not 100% certain of the accurate answer, it may show. Just a slight flicker in the eyes or a tiny twitch of the face, a fractional delay in responding, maybe a caveat to protect herself from any inaccuracies ('I think', 'I'm not certain but'). Probably such small things that nobody consciously notices but subconsciously they do – and unconsciously they compare this woman to a man in the room, who is equally uncertain of the precise answer (potentially a lot less certain than the woman) but is more comfortable with guessing. He knows that his answer is in the right ballpark, that this is good enough, and he gives it with confidence, a strong voice and no caveats. The other people in the room may not realise it at the time, or ever, but these moments are filed away somewhere. And they accumulate over time so that, one day, when they are asked to make an appointment or promotion, they just feel that the man is that bit better than the woman and therefore that he is the better candidate for a job. But what in reality is happening here has nothing to do with which of the two is better. In most instances, the bosses hardly ever know the actual answer to their question or how close a person's answer was in the meeting. (And, from experience, I can't tell you how many times I found out afterwards how accurate the women were and how far away the men were.) The accuracy or competence isn't what's noticed here. What is noticed is the confidence and self-assurance of the man versus the woman.

Confidence is something we all hugely value in people; at a profound level we believe that if a person is, or seems to be, confident, then we can have confidence in them – and vice versa. We cannot have confidence in someone who doesn't seem confident in themselves. So, every time a woman hesitates because she doesn't like guessing and inaccuracy, she projects a lack of confidence and loses a little of the confidence of those around her. And every time a man gives an answer, even an incorrect answer, and projects it confidently, he gains the confidence of others. And one day he gets the job or promotion over that woman, when he is possibly not the most competent candidate.

As an aside here, some believe that this lack of confidence and certainty can be a positive driver for women as much as it is an issue. Author Farrah Storr says that it could actually, if channelled right, give women a competitive edge:

> [It] is the reason women are proven to have a more proactive approach to learning… It is why we take less risks and why women's investment returns outperform men's… a self-checking gauge that delivers excellence… It means we prepare, question and delve deeper into problems… it is a control valve that alerts us when we are in our discomfort zone… this is where accelerated growth happens… and that's when we make true breakthroughs.

She encourages women to:

> Convert fear into excitement… Tell yourself you're
> excited, not nervous… see it as a sign you're in your
> challenge state… your discomfort zone… growing.
> This is exactly how it should feel.[18]

If women can embrace this mindset, it can help them to feel more confident and thus project more confidence. This can only benefit them as it is a natural reaction to associate confidence with competence and leadership – until we project confidence as well as men, this is a disadvantage for us and an advantage for them.

So why do many women feel less confident than men? Where does the imposter syndrome originate? One theory is that it all goes back to our school days. At school, girls are generally more sensitive to negative feedback and criticism. They learn they are in favour when they do things neatly, perfectly and quietly. When they do their work beautifully, they get A grades and praise. They like this feeling and they learn to avoid taking risks and making mistakes, which might lead to them not getting perfect marks.

At the same time, the boys are learning a different lesson at school. They generally put less focus on delivering perfect work and generally tend not to sit quietly and obediently in the classroom, so as a result they absorb significantly more scolding and punishment from their teachers than the girls do. Unlike most girls, they get used to being shouted at regularly, and they therefore become somewhat numbed to it and learn to take failure and imperfection in their stride. Studies have shown that boys absorb as much as eight times the criticism for their conduct as girls do.[19] That means eight times more experience of imperfection and eight times more opportunities to learn that being imperfect isn't an issue. As a result, they are a lot less afraid of failure and imperfection than girls – and this unconscious feeling that is learnt as a child stays with them through their lives and presents itself as confidence, or lack of it, in the workplace.

Thus the 'School Legacy' is not necessarily a positive one for girls as they become women and enter the world of work. As author Carol Dweck says:

> If life were one long grade school, women would be the undisputed rulers of the world... They leave school crammed with historical facts... proud of their ability to study hard and get the grades... They slam into a work world that doesn't reward them for perfect spelling.[20]

In financier and campaigner Dame Helena Morrissey's words,

> developing a great career is not like passing an exam. There is no test date, no objective assessment, no certificate... We need to prepare young women for that.[21]

While girls are training to win at school, the boys are training to win at life because there is no such thing as perfection in the real working world. There are no A grades for getting all the answers right because there are often no right or wrong answers. The woman who is hesitating and waiting to be certain is going to lose out to a man who has learnt, since he was a small boy, that there is nothing to lose by throwing things out there. In a world where perfection does not exist, the perfectionist is going to feel, and look, anxious and unconfident, while the one who never expected to achieve perfection is going to look confident, self-assured – like a leader.

There is a further layer to be aware of when we consider the issue of confidence: research has consistently shown that the presence of men undermines women's confidence and results in a drop in their performance. One study ran a mathematics test in groups of three with some mixed-gender groups and some all-female groups. They found that women did significantly worse in the presence of men.[22]

Again, this phenomenon begins in our childhood days. There are numerous studies from all over the world which show that girls perform better in single-sex schools versus mixed. One study found that the higher the percentage of girls in a co-ed classroom, the better the academic performance and another study found that converting from single-sex to co-ed leads to falling academic results (for all students in fact, both male and female).[23] A national study from UCLA perceived girls from single-sex schools have an edge over their co-ed peers.[24] A 2017 study of Years 3, 5 and 7 numeracy and literacy data by Dr Katharine Dix of the Australian Council for Educational Research found that, even when socio-economic status was taken into account, Year 7 girls at single-sex schools were 4.2 terms ahead of co-ed students in reading and 2.8 terms ahead in maths.[25] A 2015 experiment was run in Swiss high schools by Gerald Eisenkopf, which identified a clear positive effect on the mathematics proficiency of girls randomly assigned to single-sex schools – the girls also evaluated their own maths skills more positively.[26] An analysis of 2015 UK GCSE results showed that 75% of girls attending state girls schools achieved five good GCSEs, while only 55% of those attending co-ed schools achieved the same (the analysis did adjust for socio-economic background and selective intake).[27] In a 2012 study by Hyunjoon Park, Jere Behrman and Jaesung Choi of South Korean students, girls attending single-sex high schools presented significantly higher average scores than their peers in co-ed schools.[28] Again in 2012, Dana Diaconu's PhD thesis showed statistically significantly higher scores in science for girls from single-sex schools in Hong Kong and New Zealand.[29] Professor Alison Booth of the Australian National University found that even just one hour a week of single-sex education benefits girls and, in her 2013 study, found that female students at the University of Essex who were randomly assigned to all-female classes in their first year were 7% more likely to pass their introductory course and scored 8% higher in their final examinations.[30] The consistent learning is that, in mixed classes, boys often put girls down when they are trying to express an idea. In a single-sex environment, they feel less shy and more confident, which means they are more willing to ask for help and less afraid to try things out, so will take more risks. Perhaps it is not surprising then that, when we look at the best performing schools in England, over 70% are single-sex girls schools.[31] This gives us a pretty clear indication of what girls and women can deliver when they are unleashed from the negative effect of male presence on their confidence and performance.

So with this in mind, let's consider a hypothetical workplace meeting. There are men and women in the meeting but, as is often the case, the men significantly outnumber the women. A key business issue is being discussed, points of view are being shared, difficult questions are being asked. Based on all of the research above, what we will witness is a double whammy confidence effect – the men will, in general, feel more confident expressing their views and handling questions; but the women will feel even less confident in themselves, not just because of the presence of the men, but because of their dominant presence in numbers.

As we consider our formative years, there is also little doubt that participation in sport plays a big role in the development of children. There is a large body of evidence linking female participation in sport to personal and career success. It is proven that girls and women who play sport have more self-confidence and are more likely to go to and graduate from college, find a job and be employed in male-dominated industries.[32]

In a survey of 821 high-level executives, 90% of women played sports – and among women currently holding a top c-suite position, this proportion rose to 96% and the average salary of women who have played sport is 7% higher than those who have not.[33] However, the data shows that girls are six times more likely to drop out of playing sport than boys and, by age 15, only 15% of girls are playing sport versus 30% of boys.[34] This is extremely important because sport teaches and embeds some key skills – leadership and teamwork, of course, but also the confidence and resilience that comes from failure and perseverance. Playing sport may also help develop men's generally healthy attitude to competition (that your competitor's success is *not* a reflection on you) that comes from self-confidence, versus the less healthy female attitude (that your competitor's success is your failure). Sport teaches us how to win but also how to lose and keep going; from sport we discover that losing is normal, something to learn and bounce back from. Sport is a mini-version of life and playing sport, with all its ups and downs, is training for life and for work. And, in today's world, boys are getting significantly more of this training than girls are.

There are many reasons why girls drop out of sport. Ironically, lack of confidence and fear of failure is one of the most common, showing a lack of the very confidence and ability to deal with failure that sport would teach them! Perhaps unsurprisingly, girls and women generally don't enjoy playing sports with boys and men. In a recent survey in Switzerland, 35% of women said they prefer female-only sports. This is probably linked to the fact that 30% of the women who responded to the survey said they had witnessed sexist remarks or gestures in sport, with 26% having been victims of this themselves.[35] But I suspect there are other reasons too, potentially including a wish to escape, once in a while, from a culture or activity that is male-dominated.

It also isn't just from participation in official sports that boys are gaining an advantage in their development – from a very young age, boys are also learning from the way they play. They tease and roughhouse each other a lot more than girls do, so being insulted and attacked comes to have less impact on them (and, recall from the chapter on science, hormonally they are already less prone to sensitivity). This ability to stay strong in the face of attack is another male secret weapon in the workplace. Who would not have more confidence in the robust man versus the more 'sensitive and emotional' woman who, when she is attacked or challenged, cannot hide her slightly trembling lip and moist eyes?

I had my eyes opened to an even more extreme version of this a couple of years ago. I was on a MARC Gender Diversity training course where the men and the women learnt a lot of things they didn't know about each other. (One eye-opening realisation for the men was that all the women in the group get their house keys ready before they get to their house so they can open the door quickly and minimise the time a potential attacker has to get to them before they are safely inside.) But perhaps the biggest insight I got from this training course about men was that every single one of them had been in a physical fight of some kind at some point in their life, versus a very small number of the women. Now this is, of course, a horrible thing for boys and men to experience. But what they told us is that it has taught them the reality of being hit and, thus, they are not paralysed by the fear of it. This is unlike women who, thankfully, are less likely to have experienced physical violence and therefore are afraid of the threat of it. So, if we think about it from a man's point of view, verbal criticism or an interrogative attack at work mustn't, in comparison, seem very threatening at all and he isn't going to break or lose his confident presence because of it.

What is important is that men's confidence is genuine and honest. When they rate themselves ahead of their abilities, they really believe it. When they apply for a job they are not fully qualified for, it is because they really believe they can do it. They are not faking their confidence in themselves and we know how important that is, because we have seen how critical it is for people to seem authentic to foster confidence.

Having said all of this about men generally having more underlying confidence in themselves than women, I don't believe that anyone (women or men) has total self-confidence all the time. As trade unionist Doreen Bogdan-Martin told me, 'The big secret is *no one* ever feels 100% prepared.'

I recently attended an after dinner speech as part of a Cranfield University training by Hattie Llewelyn-Davies, the

Chair for Housing and Homelessness and the *Sunday Times'* Non-Executive Director of the Year 2018/19. She talked about her frustration with a woman on her team, who was very capable but always apologised for a 'stupid point' she had made. As a result, she came across as unconfident and unimpressive. I asked Hattie how she had avoided falling into the classic woman trap of doing this – she said that, of course she feels nervous, scared and under-qualified sometimes, but she realised long ago that 'it's all a performance' and she can in any situation choose to present the best version of herself.

I wasn't sure how I felt about this; should we not want a world in which we can be our authentic selves and succeed without putting on a performance? But then I asked the men around me what they thought – they said, of course it's a performance! They shared that they get nervous and intimidated sometimes too, but when they do, they take a deep breath and put on a show. (In fact, I got the sense that they thought that women were a bit dim if they didn't realise this was necessary sometimes.) It was a new insight for me that men may not always be as confident as they seem in these moments. This realisation highlights yet another layer in all of this: it is not just underlying confidence that is important but also the ability to put on a confident performance (delivered authentically) even when you have a few inevitable doubts. Why, then, is this something men generally do better than women? Perhaps it is because they understand and accept early on in life that

> The closer you get to the summit of success, the more you realise everyone is winging it.[36]

They become more practised at delivering the performance, with more experience and role models who do know how to wing it and to perform.

I think the key is that most men are, and appear, more confident than women, not because they know more (or feel that they do), but because they are more comfortable with *not* knowing. They are used to not knowing from an early age, they know that it is not possible to know everything ('The more you know, the more you don't know,' as Aristotle said). They know that nobody is perfect, nobody has all the answers; they don't expect this of themselves and they don't believe anyone else expects it of them either. And because they are comfortable with that knowledge, they are confident – and confidence looks like leadership. So we see that 'women have misunderstood an important law of the professional jungle'[37] and that there is an important confidence versus competence equation at play: confidence is as important if not more important than competence and a person's success correlates as closely with their confidence as it does with their competence. As career coach and author Dr Lois P Frankel says, 'Competence is only table stakes [the bare minimum] – competence alone won't move you forwards.'[38]

The issue in all of this is that we all admire, reward and promote the confident leader but confident doesn't mean better. In fact, the bigger issue is that the confident male leader may not be as good as his female rivals, and it could even mean he's a lot worse. This causes people with lower competence to get the jobs or promotions over competent women, which results in worse performance for the business – and I don't think anybody wants this. This explains why author and businessman James Collins is very wary of leaders with 'the liability of charisma'[39] and psychologist and author Tomas Chamorro-Premuzic goes as far as to believe that confidence can be a negative:

Traits like overconfidence… should be seen as red flags… They prompt us to say: Ah, there's a charismatic fellow! He's probably leadership material… It is this mistaken insistence that con- fidence equates to greatness that is the reason so many ill-suited men get top jobs. The result in both business and politics is a surplus of incompetent men in charge, and this surplus reduces opportunities for competent people – women and men.[40]

He makes a convincing case for a more modest, less 'in your face' confident style of leader such as Angela Merkel, who he describes as the 'most boring and best leader' in politics.[41] US investment banker Fiona Grieg has said that, in her experience, a candidate's assertiveness had nothing to do with his or her performance but that the more assertive candidates, not necessarily the best, were being promoted.[42] We talked earlier about how we all value gravitas, but the question is – do we want someone who has weight in their words, or weight in what they do? Under-qualified, over-confident men are moving up and over-qualified, under-confident women are being held back, which leads to inefficiency and lower performance in the workplace.[43] Too often we mistake a woman's meekness for weakness and we give the job that should, based on ability, be hers to a more confident but less competent man.

People talk about there being a glass ceiling for women. But the ceiling isn't glass. You can see glass; you can touch it. This is the Invisible Ceiling, the invisible power of culture – unconscious bias and confidence. The ceiling women hit is worse than a glass one, it is invisible. But it is there and women can feel it. It may have taken some time and experience for some of us but we feel it – and it's the job of those who feel it first to make it visible so we can start to remove it.

8

Giving good meeting

ONE OF THE most obvious and important places that we see a person's confidence (and thus judge their competence and leadership) is in 'the meeting'. And my goodness you have got to give it to them, some men know how to give good meeting! If it were possible to keep score of how men and women perform and present themselves in meetings across the world, whether in the workplace or at the local school or charity committee, men would win virtually every game and would hardly concede a goal in the process.

Let's face some realities. For many people, the place where they are seen in action by their boss, or by people who influence their career, is in the meeting room. Most bosses don't tend to work-shadow their employees and watch how well they are handling phone calls or writing emails. The place they usually interact with their employees is in a meeting. Men know that to win at work they need to win at meetings, and they know how.

So how do you win at meetings?

First, you need to speak – and speak up early. Research shows that the first or second person who speaks in a meeting sets and controls the agenda. And we know that speaking up in discussions is something men generally do more easily than women. A Harvard Study of first year MBA students showed that women are significantly less likely to contribute in classes and lectures[1] and, even in the Swedish Parliament which is 40% female, women give fewer speeches than men. Kate Fall, who was ex-PM David Cameron's Deputy Chief of Staff says she found it 'daunting' speaking up in meetings full of alpha males. This is not, of course, to say that women never speak up and speak well. I worked for a highly impressive and successful woman and what set her apart was not her high intelligence and great talent (though she had this of course) but her outstanding communication skills. She spoke with great confidence, gave self-assured responses and held the floor in meetings in a way that most women I have seen do not. Thatcher would have approved.

Because it's not just about saying something in meetings. and making a point quickly and succinctly – you need to be comfortable to speak at length sometimes. I used to observe men in meetings, holding the floor for ten minutes or more while they shared four or five points. And I realised that I had never seen a woman do this in a meeting, unless she was the Chairperson or presenter. In the words of Professor of Linguistics Deborah Tannen:

> Women often feel they don't want to take up more
> space than necessary, so they'll often be more succinct.[2]

The irony is that taking up this space and time in the meeting often gets people noticed and listened to more than brevity and clarity does. Virtually every woman on the planet will tell you that she has had the experience(s) of making an excellent, clear and succinct point in a meeting and felt that it had not really been heard, only to hear a man repeat it in a different (and usually much more long-winded) way later and be told what an excellent point it is. Women get frustrated that the man has 'stolen' her point or idea, when in reality it is more likely that nobody even heard or registered it when she said it – because she wasn't able to make it in the way it needed to be made to be impactful in that environment, whereas the man was (although of course he had the advantage over her that he is a man and taken more seriously).

The added problem is that, with all this expansive talking

going on in meetings, it is a challenge to get a word in edgeways. Women want to make a point, and we know that we should, because why be there if we are going to stay quiet – as author Laura Liswood says: 'If you can't communicate, you can't lead.'[3] The issue is that most men are naturally more comfortable challenging and interrupting and most women prefer to wait for others to finish their points and then have their turn to speak uninterrupted. But this is, unfortunately, a moment which, from experience, may never come. A 2019 survey of 329 companies by McKinsey and LeanIn.org found that half of the women surveyed had experienced being interrupted or spoken over.[4] Regrettably, men are also more likely to interrupt women than they are men and even view it as a power trait. Ben Barres, who is a transgender man, found he was interrupted much less than when he was female (and exactly the same presentation was perceived as better!).[5] Trade unionist and businesswoman Doreen Bogdan-Martin told me that she believes this habit comes from the reality that many men have been raised to not really listen when women are speaking. The issue then is that women, or other non-dominant group members, are put off from sharing their points again if they were interrupted the first time and so men keep the airtime, dominate the meeting – and win. On top of all this, it's not enough to speak early, at length and frequently, if we want to 'give good meeting' we also need to speak strongly, loudly and with expansive body language. Yes, to win at meetings we women may also need a testosterone injection beforehand, or to become an actual man. It is extremely difficult for women to authentically do some of the things that are valued in meetings.

This is all, of course, driven by the male-dominant culture in male-dominated meetings; you will see something very different in a gender balanced or female-dominated group. I recently attended a training course run by two women in which 80% or more of the participants were female. It was fascinating to see women in this environment, speaking with total confidence, happily holding the floor at length to express points, getting at least their fair share of voice. Importantly, everyone (men and women) was fully participating and listening to each other so everybody's input and thoughts were being heard. Absolute. Meeting. Bliss.

What has not been meeting bliss for most women, however, is virtual meetings. The significant shift to these as a result of the Covid-19 crisis has been another issue to deal with. If interruptions and trying to get a word in edgeways were challenges before, they have become even more of a problem in the world of video calls. Perhaps not surprisingly, men know how to give good virtual meeting too.

While we do sometimes have a good laugh about the way men act in male-dominant meetings and have some funny names for it (the 'Manologue', the 'Hepeat', 'Acquired Definite Answer Syndrome'), it's extremely important. When men are dominating, winning the meeting, and women are quiet, it means that vital points are not being made or heard that should be. This restricts and limits the input to, and content of, the meeting and affects the quality of the decisions taken and actions agreed as a result. These poor quality decisions in turn weaken the performance of the business. There was a classic example of this in a round table political discussion on abortion with one woman and three men. The men consistently cut the woman off and told her to hold on as she tried to get a word in edgeways. Yes, the one woman in a meeting on abortion didn't even get to speak on the subject. Think of how many discussions happen around the world every day where women's important points of view are not made or heard.

And it goes beyond this too, because 'giving good meeting' looks and feels like leadership to us. So, how a man or woman performs in meetings is a huge contributor to how he or she is perceived and whether or not he or she is considered the right candidate for a role or promotion. As with confidence in general, winning at meetings has absolutely nothing to do with how competent or how capable a leader a person is. But bad decisions about people are made based on these things, which ultimately means these are bad decisions for the business. As Carolyn Tastad, Group President of North America for P&G, says, for companies to instil change, 'We need to expand our definition of what leadership looks like.'[6]

So to all the men out there, I ask you to think about this next time you are in a meeting. If you see a woman typing away at her laptop instead of participating passionately in the discussion, it is more likely not that she has nothing to contribute but that she has tried to be heard, failed to be heard, got bored of listening to all the men on their soapboxes and decided a much better use of her time would be to finish that important document that she needs to get out. Don't assume she doesn't have something important to say – ask her what she thinks, she might just have a gem of an insight for you. Just because someone is staying quiet doesn't mean they're not brilliant.

9

The umbrella theory

WE'RE ALL TOLD a lot of fairy-tales when we are young. But, as time goes on, we come to realise that Father Christmas hasn't really been coming down our chimney every year and we're probably not going to be rescued from a tower by a handsome prince one day. Yet, one of the things many of us continue to believe well into our adult life is the 'myth of meritocracy'. We need to face the brutal reality that meritocracy – recognition and promotions based solely on performance and merit – is just that, a myth. If society really was a meritocracy, we would be at 50/50 gender representation in everything, including in all senior roles, including CEO, because women are as competent, intelligent and capable as men. The people who don't understand that meritocracy is a myth, and act accordingly, are at a serious career disadvantage.

The problem is that virtually every woman I ever managed or mentored believed in the myth of meritocracy. In general, women think that if they do a good job, that is enough – and when I have told men this, I have seen them either laugh out loud or look completely incredulous and say, 'You're joking, right?'

I'm afraid I'm not. I cannot tell you how many times over 25 years in management I have heard a woman say the same thing:

> If I work hard and deliver the results, the rest will come. My company will look after me and my career will look after itself.

Women believe that if they do a great job, this will be seen and recognised and rewarded automatically – that their work will speak for itself. But, as Carla Harris, Vice Chairman of Morgan Stanley, says, 'absolute meritocracy doesn't exist when humans are involved.'[1]

Men are, in general, much more savvy about this. They know that the world isn't watching them most of the time, so if they want someone to notice their work and their brilliance, they need to make sure it is visible to the people that matter. Men understand that self-marketing and 'image management' is very necessary and are brought up to know that the squeaky wheel gets the grease. Their meeting contributions and speeches are a part of delivering this, but their self-marketing strategy goes a lot further.

The next problem here is that virtually all of the women I have met absolutely loathe the concept of self-marketing and are very uncomfortable doing it. They are also more reluctant than men to push themselves forwards and state their ambitions. So, they either avoid doing it or, if they do force themselves to, they often come over as awkward and inauthentic (because they are not being true to their personality). This, of course, is never going to impress the person they are targeting, who will subconsciously pick up on the inauthenticity.

Meanwhile the men are comfortable self-marketing away, so their work is much more visible to their managers and much more likely to be recognised and rewarded (with a bigger salary, a better job, a promotion). This is especially frustrating for women when they know that the man's work is no better than theirs, or even not as good, and he still gets the job she feels she deserves. And it's worse at the top levels. One Fortune 500 c-suite executive felt she lost out to a man who hadn't 'made his numbers in seven years'[2] and Ellen Kullman, former Chief Executive of DuPont, says:

> I think we tend to be brought up thinking that life's
> fair, that you thrive and deliver, and the rest will take

care of itself. It actually does work for most of your career. It doesn't work for that last couple of steps.[3]

One of the things I say to women I have coached is that yes, maybe in an ideal world, our bosses would spend their working days not actually doing any of their own work but just observing us, sitting in on our meetings, analysing our discussions and emails and marvelling at how brilliant we are. But that is not going to happen – and nor should it. This would be a personal coach, not a manager who has things to contribute in their own right. I tell them about 'The Umbrella Theory', that we all need to think about ourselves as working under open umbrellas with our bosses sitting above us – all they can see is the tops of the umbrellas, not what is going on underneath. They are only able to see what is happening underneath if one of three things happen: one, they are alerted to a problem or crisis under the umbrellas so they come under to check things out (bad); two, they are a superb people manager with excess time on their hands because they don't have much to do so they regularly check in spontaneously on what their reports are doing (these are very rare, you're lucky you if you have one); three, you invite your boss to take a look underneath your umbrella at what you are working on (self-marketing in other words). I think it's pretty obvious which of these three is the most appealing, likely scenario.

One thing to be aware of is that ensuring your work is visible becomes more and more necessary as you become more senior in an organisation. I certainly experienced this. When we are at a more junior level, we are to an extent an 'apprentice' and our boss does spend more time with us, watching us, coaching us – and our boss is also still relatively junior, so they have less pressure than a senior manager would have and often more time to spend with us. So, at the more junior levels, our work and our talent and ability are naturally more visible to our bosses, without us having to make any effort to self-market or self-promote. At this level, therefore, just doing a great job can actually be enough; the recognition and rewards come naturally, and the career does, to an extent, look after itself.

However, as we get more senior, things are not like this at all. Our seniority grows and with it (rightly) the percentage of our working time that is spent entirely separate and independent from our boss. He (yes, I'm going to stick my neck out and say it's a 'he') isn't there to see our skilful management of that sales meeting or our insightful strategic interventions – he has virtually no visibility of what we are doing or how we are doing it, unless we make a conscious effort to show him. If we are not careful, all he will see is our results and I can promise you this is not enough. I have seen many examples where people with mediocre or poor results have been promoted ahead of others with excellent results because they have invested in and done a much better job of communicating with their management, ensuring the context of their work is understood. I have many times heard it said that a man's weaker results looked stronger because of the difficult situation they faced in producing them. And as Laura Liswood says,

> [the] ingrained inclination is to give the benefit to the one who has kept them updated and subtly bragged about their work.[4]

I remember when I was a Marketing Director, I saw the male Marketing Directors around me constantly calling out business crises and setting up urgent meetings with the Country General Manager to work through them. I was looking on thinking, frankly, it was all a bit pathetic and that these were hardly what I would call crises – I was facing similar issues all the time and dealing with them myself, with my team, without having to bother my General Manager with them. I prided myself on the fact that I virtually never had to disturb him or ask him for help. I believed that success for me was to handle everything and keep him free to manage other things. So it was a bit of a shock for me when it came to review time at the end of the year – my results were excellent, double-digit growth and way ahead of the other business units, but I came out nowhere near the top of the pile because my boss felt that 'my job had been a lot easier than that of my peers'. Because he had seen they had had a lot of crises to manage that he had needed to help with, he valued their contribution more highly. It was then that I realised that what my male peers had been doing with those 'pathetic' crisis meetings was making their work and their contribution visible (and also, by the way, making my boss feel needed and able to contribute, which is of course something all human beings want to feel). Meanwhile, I had been shutting him out and hiding my contributions away under my umbrella.

So, I learnt some big lessons about the reality of the workplace – it is not enough, not by a long way, just to get on with your job quietly and well. I don't believe this will ever really change completely, as no manager can always get a completely clear picture of who is doing (or not doing...) what. However, this isn't an excuse for those people who only focus on managing up and don't do much work under the umbrella. You know who you are. And it isn't an excuse for managers who are too dumb to notice that they are being conned by these people. You need to be regularly looking under the umbrellas to see who is really 'getting shit done' (as my brilliant colleague and friend Janet Allgaier used to say) and who is just focusing on making you think they are. It's not for no reason that GALLUP® found that

The traditional annual performance review is one of the most dreaded activities in the workplace. Employees complain that these meetings are unfair, biased and superficial.[5]

Look around and you will see too many men doing a lot of talk and not a lot of actual work, and a lot of women shaking their heads in quiet frustration and clearing up. My female

CMO friend accepted that her previous Managing Director, in her words, 'does F all but talks very well'.

And now onto networking – another word that send shivers down the spine of many women. Over the course of my career I have come across maybe a couple of women who were pretty comfortable with doing it, but I have discussed networking with hundreds who absolutely hate it. They hate that they should have to do it (because they believe in the myth of meritocracy and that their work should speak for itself) and they hate actually doing it because they find it really uncomfortable and don't know how to initiate or manage the discussion. Talking with a boss or senior in a work context about something that isn't directly their work but simply about them and their career feels very unnatural and like a poor use of everyone's time. One woman even described it to me as 'brazen' and the career equivalent of walking up to a man in a bar and asking him out. Now men, you may not understand this discomfort and you may find it ridiculous – but I promise you it's very real in most of the women you have worked with and will work with. You need to know that a woman not discussing her career with you doesn't mean it's not important to her and it doesn't mean you should dismiss her as a strong talent.

I heard a perfect example of this recently from a senior male manager I know well and whose people skills I have a lot of admiration for. He had managed one woman for many years and told me that he thought she was excellent at her job but that she had never, in all the time she had worked for him, even when prompted, shared any wish to progress or move into another role. He told me that he had got to the point where this was making him seriously question her – not just her lack of career ambition but her ability in general. In his mind, if someone doesn't show proactiveness about their career then they can't be proactive in their job. This was a huge insight for me – men value ambition enormously, they value people who want to move upwards and forwards. For them, staying still and being happy to do a great job in the job we're in isn't enough and they think less of others for it – even though some women feel this is ridiculous. So, take note – when you don't discuss your career and what you want for it with your boss or senior, they don't just think you're not proactive about your career, they think you aren't proactive at all. Your lack of self-promotion and networking isn't just stopping your work being visible, it's actually undermining the perception of your work – and of you.

Another thing men know is that access to your manager is critical because as humans we are naturally and unconsciously more inclined to turn to the people we know and with whom we are comfortable. Unlike women, who often skip lunch because they don't have enough time, men see all this as the opposite of a waste of time; they know that lunch is the most important meeting of the day and that 'Golf is simply another word for access.'[6] One COO noticed that only men 'wandered' past his office – which was at the end of a corridor![7] Quite simply, most men know something that many women do not, as Vivian Giang summarises:

> Many high achievers, especially women, believe
> that their work will speak for itself, but absolute
> meritocracy doesn't exist when humans are involved.[8]

Even highly successful women struggle with this. Jan Fields, ex-President of McDonald's in the US, has said that she rose fastest when measured by straightforward metrics such as profit.[9] While women focus on building their performance, men are also building their 'relationship currency', which is a critical invisible force in gaining sponsorship and support for a key role or promotion. In *Strategize to Win*, Carla Harris, Vice Chairman at Morgan Stanley, explains that attracting a sponsor takes more than doing good work:

> It might not be enough currency to win the next

level of trust... good work will get you on a shortlist
of names, but the work alone – that performance
currency – isn't enough for someone to speak up
on your behalf when your name is called from that
list behind closed doors. For that to happen, you
need relationship currency, or the one people find
they don't have time for because they're too busy
generating performance currency... The sponsor uses
their own hard-earned capital to influence someone
else's judgement on your behalf... the sponsor now
feels they know you beyond your... work, enough to
endorse you. Your relationship currency allows you to
buy access... This requires taking the time and effort.[10]

This is a big reminder to many women that, no matter how
much time and effort they put into their work, they will never
be rewarded as they feel they deserve to be if they are not
being smart about how humans make important decisions.

One thing we can't ignore though about networking and
building 'relationship currency' is that women's dislike of it is
not the only reason they don't tend to do it – in general, they
also have less available time in the working day to do it. Here
we are, well into the 21st century and women, even if they are
in a full-time job, even if they are earning as much as or more as
their husband or partner, they are also virtually always COOS
of the home and are carrying the majority of the domestic
workload – including childcare. A Bureau of Labor Statistics
American Time Use Survey found that 85% of women versus
67% of men spend some time doing household activities in an
average day, with women spending an average of 2.6 hours
versus men spending 2.1 hours on these; when averaged over
the course of a week, women spend 16.1 hours caring for and
helping household members and men spend 11.2 hours.[11]
An extensive global survey by the Boston Consulting Group
found that women take 88% of the responsibility for grocery
shopping, 84% for meal preparations, 84% for laundry, 80%

for cleaning, and 76% for admin.[12] Women spend on average 16 hours per week on household chores, and 38% say their husbands or live-in partners do virtually no household chores (ranging from 74% in Japan, 40% in the UK, 34% in the US to 29% in India). Meanwhile, German and French women shoulder 93% of household duties.[13]

I was naively optimistic at the beginning of the Covid-19 lockdown, I thought that it may be a catalyst for this to change. Surely when more men started working from home, they would become more aware of the amount of household work and childcare their female partner does and step up to share the load? Unfortunately, this was not the case, as many surveys showed (including my own). LeanIn.org found that 77% of mothers had taken on even more household work than before and that, concerningly, 25% of women in a full-time job with a partner and kids were experiencing severe anxiety (compared with 11% of men).[14] In a *New York Times* poll, 80% of women said they were fully or mostly responsible for the housework and home schooling and 70% for the childcare.[15]

A female CEO friend of mine with a partner and kids told me what her days looked like, starting with breakfast at 7am, then a morning of home schooling, lunch preparations, an afternoon of work calls, dinner preparations and bedtime, then working on the laptop until midnight. It was clear that I had been too optimistic, and most men were not stepping up.

Men are nearly four times more likely than women to have a partner who assumes the primary responsibility for the household and children. One consequence of this is that men are able to work more hours per week than women. A GALLUP® report from 2016 showed that managers believed that the people who were in the office putting in more face time were better performers[16] and that, in this context, 47% of men said they worked more than 40 hours per week, while 30% of women said the same. 'Perceptions of time spent in the office can also suppress women's pay cheques as well as their opportunities for business and career growth.'[17]

Even before Covid-19, women were frequently burnt out and pushed to their physical limits, often due to sleep deprivation; working mums get the least sleep, with 59% of respondents in a national survey reporting sleep deprivation – which led Arianna Huffington to declare 'sleep as a feminist issue'.[18] Women, as a result, are more likely than men to suffer poor health due to excessive work-related stress.

A study at Duke University found higher stress levels and a greater risk of heart disease in women than men – and sometimes even leading to mental health problems.[19] Women in the UK are 53% more stressed at work than men – for men, the rate was 1,270 cases per 100,000 workers; for women it was nearly double that, at 2,250 cases.[20] We can understand why a job or career can become simply unsustainable for a woman in the long-term, if the combination of her 'paid work' and her 'unpaid family work' has got to the point of impacting her physical and mental health. It is not that women are not willing to put the hours in to do a high-level job, but they have their limits. GALLUP® found that 79% of women would not be discouraged by working 50 hours a week, but 72% would be discouraged from pursuing a high-level job with a 60 hour working week.[21] This is probably because they know it's not sustainable because they have too much else to bloomin' well do! One widely-shared post on Instagram sums up the issue:

> We expect women to work as if they don't have
> children, and to raise children as if they don't work.[22]

As a result of all this, we start to understand why women find less time to network than men. Even if we could take away all of the invisible forces of culture and confidence, it is still just not physically possible for women to have the time to do everything. It is easier for most men to fit in that networking coffee or lunch and know they can stay on a bit later that evening if necessary, to finish off anything that they need to get out of the door. Many women will have a hard deadline for leaving (for the school pick-up or the nanny) and they feel they need to prioritise getting their work done before they go ahead of a networking chat that they believe is lower priority and certainly not urgent.

One of my big frustrations when talking about gender diversity issues is how quickly people always make the jump from registering that women are carrying the majority of the household work and childcare responsibilities to discussing flexi-work policies and crèche facilities. As if this will miraculously fix all the issues that women face as they try to progress their career. Now, don't get me wrong, this is an area where a lot more needs to be done. Thirty-three per cent of working mothers say their employer is doing 'very poorly' at allowing them to work from home when needed, 20% of women say their employer is doing 'somewhat well', 'poorly' or 'very poorly' at providing any flexible working arrangements.[23] And the men who do want to carry their share of the burden are not getting a lot of support. In a survey of 2,000 British men aged 24–40, 63% had requested a change to their working patterns since becoming a father and 44% were turned down.[24]

The two men I know who have taken paid paternity leave have faced major piss-taking from male colleagues, with the implication that they will be in cafés 'drinking lattes' all day. One was made to feel by his boss that his job is too important for him to be taking time out, to the point that he even considered 'hiding' his paternity leave as a sabbatical. Thankfully, he had the courage to not do this and has declared the experience 'life-changing', 'exhausting' and one that has given him a new respect for his wife that he will never forget. (As an aside, isn't it interesting that we all accept women taking time out of their important jobs for maternity leave? Are the men's jobs more important then, or are the men doing their important jobs in a more important way than women are and not expected to take time out for their newborn children?)

This was also highlighted during the Covid-19 lockdown, with some fathers telling me that they did want to step up and share the housework and childcare but they did not receive any support from their employers, who assumed they had a wife and that she would take care of that while he continued to hit all his work deadlines. As a result, men's careers were prioritised and women and their careers suffered, with significantly higher job losses during and after the crisis amongst women than men.[25] But this issue was not caused by Covid-19, it was there long before – what 2020 taught us is that the careers of women with families were houses built on weak foundations, with women carrying too much of the unpaid work and trying to manage everything – they were already at their limit and this brought the house crashing down. Moving forward, we need to build a more robust system for parents (not just mums) to ensure the load is manageable and their work-life balance is sustainable.

So yes, there is a lot of work to do here to ensure the load is shared and not too heavy for women. And flexible employer policies clearly help – but it is far from the only solution needed to drive gender diversity. The domestic load on women is also a lot more visible and address-able than the other greater problems, so there is a tendency for some companies to focus on this issue with a few policies and then feel it is 'job done' on the gender equality front – when there is so much more complex stuff going on that affects women's commitment to their job and to their organisation that needs to be understood and addressed. Because it is not simply the impact on their time, and thus wellbeing, that affects women and their work and careers, it is also the hidden effects of the frustration that arises from gender inequality for women at work. We know that employees who feel discriminated against are less likely to be committed to work and more likely to quit. We've also seen why women may not feel they're 'getting what they deserve' in the non-meritocratic world of work where networking and self-marketing contributes as much (if not more) to salary levels and promotion opportunities as doing a good job. On top of this, we add the extra household and family demands a woman is often dealing with and we have a real downward spiral from a gender diversity point of view. The 2017 report on women worldwide from GALLUP® and the International Labour Organization states that

> Kids are a company's greatest competition... A company's greatest competitors can be 4 feet tall with missing teeth and a soccer ball in their hands, crying in diapers, or asking to borrow the car on a Friday night.[26]

But it's not as simple as this. In fact, it's clear that women are willing to make big personal sacrifices, including time away from home and family, for jobs that they love. In the *Harvard Business Review*, Hewlett and Luce talk about the 'push and pull' factors and how they interact. They describe personal and family as 'pull factors' – because they can potentially make women feel 'pulled' away from work and career. Then there are the 'push factors', such as feeling under-utilised at work, not getting a decent salary increase, being given more responsibility without the promotion or title to go with it. They lay out that it is not the 'pull factors' alone that cause a woman to give up and leave her job but the combined force of the 'push and pull factors'. Women ask themselves, what is the point of suffering the painful 'pull factors' if I am not valued at work?[27] A GALLUP® report sums it up:

> Because of this push and pull, time spent at work has to be worthwhile... And when businesses fail to create a culture that makes sense for women, it is easier for working mothers to choose that preferred path.[28]

Data has shown that more than half of women who earn an MBA from Harvard don't end up in a full-time job.[29] Companies and organisations are losing, and will lose, talented women, women who are potentially more talented than some of the men who stay – women who would be contributing stronger results if they were to stay.

Importantly, often nobody sees this coming because a woman is likely, as we have seen, to have been less vocal and open about her career frustrations. She may have seemed to have tolerated what a man doesn't when, in fact, on the inside she is silently not tolerating it at all and even maybe taking it very personally. So, one day, without warning, she is out of the door and on her way to enjoy those inviting 'pull factors'. And let's not forget that still, in more cases than not, it is likely that a woman will have a husband or partner who can make it financially possible for her to do this, at least in the short-term.

Possibly the biggest consequence of women believing in the 'myth of meritocracy' is the salary gap. Women keep on doing their jobs with the belief that if they do their work well, they will be rewarded and things will take care of themselves, but the reality is they don't. We have seen that men get paid 16% more than women in Europe, 23% more in the US,[30] and this is a profound underlying issue for women everywhere. One example comes from Sandi Toksvig at the 2018 Women's Equality Party Conference about the economic potential of gender equality. She was asked in the Q&A if she was confident she was receiving equal pay for her role as presenter on the quiz show, QI. A very embarrassed Sandi admitted that she had discovered she was being paid 40% of the salary of her predecessor Stephen Fry. Now, I personally can get my head round her salary being a little lower than his, not because she is a woman but because he did the job for a long time (nothing wrong with scope for salary growth over the years) and he is a better known TV personality – but 40%?! Of course, one reason for Sandi's embarrassment was that she did not want to be seen to be complaining about her very nice salary when she considers herself lucky to earn so much and has a very pleasant and comfortable lifestyle. I know many women feel this way – no need to ask for more when we have plenty. But I very much doubt that most men feel the same and their view is more that 'it's not about what's enough, it's about what I deserve.'

How ironic that even the woman who founded the Women's Equality Party was not ready or able to demand an equal salary for herself. She is far from alone in this. Linda Babcock, Professor of Economics at Carnegie Mellon University, found that men initiate salary negotiations four times as often as women do – and when women do initiate the discussion, they ask for 30% less than the men do.[31] Interestingly, it has been shown that in Australia women ask for a salary increase as often as men do, but even then the men are 25% more likely to receive one.[32]

Whichever way we look at it, it is clear that meritocracy is a myth and women are held back everywhere by their belief in it. So, the combination of women who believe in meritocracy and the fact that many workplaces are non-meritocratic plays a very important role in our gender diversity challenge. Unless this is addressed, men will continue to network and self-promote and women will continue to feel uncomfortable and will avoid doing so, women will continue to not be valued as much as men and will lose out on jobs and salaries accordingly, ultimately becoming frustrated and quitting. Managers would do well to always remember that the people you know best are not always the best people. What's important about this issue isn't that we're losing women from business per se but that we lose the competence, capability and diversity of thought of those women. This is without even taking into account how much productive time male employees waste lobbying for themselves. My friend Denise and I recently had a good laugh about this. Her (male) boss had told her that day, 'You work like a man!' He obviously meant it as a compliment but she was tempted to reply by saying, 'Oh do you mean you think I spend all of my time having coffee and networking and talking about my career and creating an impression of working really hard instead of actually working on my projects?' We did chuckle about this. But, in all seriousness, if we did all work more like the woman who believes in the myth of meritocracy and so focuses on 'more working, less networking' we would see significantly more productivity and, ultimately, better results. Perhaps women need to have less faith in meritocracy and men need to have more. What is certain is that women need to be more aware of the umbrella and we all need to be more aware of the need to look under it.

IO

The women who win at work

WHAT BECAME MORE and more clear to me as I was writing this book was that there was a big question I couldn't answer: what about the women who *do* win at work? Whichever way we look at it and whatever line of work we look at (business, sport, politics, healthcare, education, media) we see a maximum of only 7% of the top leadership positions being held by women, but 7% is not zero.[1] Seven per cent means that there are *some* women out there who have made it to the top. So, I wanted to talk with these 'Super 7%' women and try to find out what sets them apart from the rest of us. They must have faced the same barriers that all women face throughout their lives and careers, so what is it that made them push through it when most women, let's face it, are ultimately defeated by it and give up. I have been lucky to interview many incredible women – CEOs and Presidents of big companies, Chairwomen, COOs, very senior women from the worlds of TV, sport and politics. Of course, they are all unique individuals and there is no single blueprint for success, but it has been fascinating to see some clear common things emerge – including some things I didn't expect to find at the offset.

The first thing I discovered is that just because a woman made it to the top does not mean she is necessarily seen as impressive. There are two categories of women who win at work – the ones that people dislike (often intensely) and the ones that people (including men) are deeply impressed by and consider the greatest leaders (of either gender) that they have worked for or with. We're going to call the first category the 'Manly Ones' and the second the 'Authentic Women'.

Let's talk first about the Manly Ones. If I'm honest, this is what I probably initially expected – that the few women who are winning at work have done it by forgetting they are a woman and behaving like a man. This would be consistent with Helena Morrissey's view that:

> These women… who have made it to the top are
> the exceptions, the ones who have mostly played
> by the rules of the existing game… are 'a transition
> generation'… still needing to mostly fit in with the
> status quo.[2]

In reality, this isn't what I have seen at all and, in fact, of all the women I talked with, I would only put one CEO (who didn't want to be named) in this category, based on her rather aggressive denial of gender having ever been an issue for her or in her company. She told me, 'I've been lucky to work for companies where gender has not been an issue… I don't wake up in the morning and think about being a woman.'

Generally, the Manly Ones are the ones who are disliked by many of the women and men I have interviewed; one man told me, when I asked him about female leaders, that he 'hates the ones who act like men and are too aggressive' and that he can't bear the ones that 'adopted male management style.' And the ever-articulate Zaid Al-Qassab, CMO of Channel 4, told me how he can't bear 'the women who get to the top by aping male behaviour – there's nothing appealing about the alpha male leadership style even in men, let alone in women.' Another man told me how obvious it is that these female leaders are 'Queen Bees' and have a poor relationship with the other women who work with and for them and have a definite 'I got here this way, tough luck if you can't or aren't prepared to do the same' attitude.

What is certainly clear is that the women who have made it by 'acting like a man' may be able to achieve short-term success for themselves but they are not the female leaders who are admired by others. They are not doing other women who would like to follow in their footsteps one day any favours (and, let's face it, the Manly Ones probably couldn't care less about that). However, if we are going to drive gender equality we absolutely need the women who make it to the top to do a great job there, to be admired and for people to say they would feel good about appointing more women in the future, rather than 'Let's not make that mistake again.' We need to move the numbers forwards, but women like this are going to cause them to move backwards.

The good news though is that most of the Super 7% women I have personally talked with are nothing like this – they are 'Authentic Women'. They don't try to be men and are loved for it by all. These women talked about the importance of always being your 'authentic self', 'staying yourself', 'using the female EQ [emotional quotient] and leveraging the authentic female in you'. Dame Cilla Snowball, ex-Chair and CEO of Abbott Mead Vickers told me, 'I never felt I had to pretend to be someone I wasn't.' Sylvie Moreau, President of Coty Professional, shared how important staying authentic was in her experience of the Coty acquisition from P&G:

> At the Coty pitch I was the authentic me and they
> chose me, it gave me the confidence to be me in the
> new role and company.

Doreen Bogdan-Martin, Director of the Telecommunication Bureau at the International Telecommunication Union (ITU) and the first woman in ITU's 153-year history to hold elected office, also talked about having been able to be herself:

> I have my own style and I've never really known how to
> approach my work any other way except to be myself.

It's the same for one respected TV presenter, who prefers to avoid any unnecessary attention and remain anonymous: 'I've been lucky enough to always be myself within the BBC.'

Interestingly, these women shatter the myth that men are threatened by and never like women in top positions – they are not just liked by men, they are hugely admired and often adored. HR officer Dennis Shuler idolised 'authentic' businesswoman Susan Arnold at P&G and then at Disney. Channel 4's Zaid Al-Qassab loves the Group Chairman and Group Chief Executive of AMV BBDO's, Dame Cilla Snowball's

> unusual style, not the bang-the-fist-on-the-table approach but an authority without parading it that is quietly impressive.

Sal Pajwani, CEO of ?What If!, is also a big fan of Snowball: 'She wears her vulnerability on her sleeve and that makes her more powerful.' Virtually every man I spoke with who works for P&G identified the softly spoken and very humble Fama Francisco as the company's most impressive female leader. She is the first Asian female President in P&G's 180-plus-year history and in no way at all made from the P&G man mould. One CMO described his female COO to me as a leader who is the

> closest to being perfect... very human, showing vul-
> nerability... She has incredible followership both up
> and down the organisation... there are a lot of people
> in the company who say they are professionally in love
> with her.

All of the men I spoke with clearly recognise what makes these women so special and impressive: 'The authentic ones are the impressive ones, leveraging their female strengths and not trying to be something they are not.' and 'The good ones act like women.' The one question mark here is whether these men are responding positively only to the 'authenticity' of these women, or to their 'feminine' behaviours. It's possible that the 'Manly Ones' are also being their authentic selves and that their behaviour is naturally more masculine. But, because it is not what we stereotypically expect, we react negatively to that behaviour. If so, I'm doing those women a disservice, but surely authenticity by definition feels authentic and positive, so if their behaviour is authentic, it should be experienced as such, even if it is unexpected in a woman.

So, the Super 7% are respected by men and women for their authenticity, and an important key to authenticity and winning at work is knowing your strengths. People flourish when they know and leverage what they are good at, but this does require strong self-awareness. This is something the Super 7% share. As Hanneke Faber, a global President at Unilever, puts it: 'I know what I'm good at, I stay away from the rest.' All the other highly successful women I spoke with also had a very clear, early awareness of their personal strengths and of the kind of environment they would succeed in: the job, the bosses, the people, the place, the culture. Dame Cilla Snowball told me, 'I worked in the right place and picked the right people to work with,' and said she knew she was at home in an agency culture where people were focused on the job, not the politics. This was similar for Tamara Ingram OBE, CEO of J Walter Thompson: 'At Saatchi I was very at home, it was my natural place to be.' Sylvie Moreau knew early on that she had strengths in operational and beauty category work and purposefully positioned herself to do a role that best matched her individual talents: 'I tilted my career to do a job I am perfect for.'

This is consistent with the CliftonStrengths® (formerly StrengthsFinder®) philosophy that the key to success in life and work is to focus on what we are naturally strong at and not spend any time or energy on the rest. One of my hypotheses about gender inequality had been that men and women may have different natural strengths. Anna Sawyer, Director and strengths expert at GALLUP®, set me straight that this is not really the case. While there are *some* differences in the strength profile of men versus women (Empathy®, Developer®, Includer® and Discipline® have higher frequency amongst women, for example),[3] Anna told me that what is important is not what your strengths are but how well you use them: it's about knowing your natural edge and turning this into your superpower. And when a person focuses on and utilises their strengths, and doesn't try to copy the behaviours of others, they are being their authentic self. As we know, being authentic also drives their sense of comfort, which drives their internal and external confidence and helps them succeed.

Tom Rath and Barry Conchie, in *Strengths-Based Leadership,* expand on this idea:

> We all lead in very different ways, based on our talents
> and our limitations… If you look at great historical
> leaders such as Winston Churchill or Mahatma Gandhi,
> you might notice more differences than similarities.[4]

But the key thing Churchill, Gandhi and the Super 7% all have in common is that they leveraged their individual dominant strengths, 'they have exceptional clarity about who they are – and who they are not.'[5] Mervyn Davies, CEO and Chairman of Standard Chartered Bank, says that 'the most important aspect of leading is simply knowing oneself.'[6] One of Rath and Conchie's examples of such a leader is Wendy Kopp, Founder and CEO of Teach for America, who has leveraged her unique strengths to create an organisation that has reached more than three million students. Rath and Conchie stress how critical it is that 'Leaders stay true to who they are.' Best Buy's Brad Anderson agrees, describing trust as 'the most cherished and valuable commodity in a work environment' and that 'the key to building trust is being authentic.' Psychotherapist and charisma coach Richard Reid believes in the importance of 'having a strong, consistent identity' because 'Charismatic people don't change to fit in.' We all know how seductive charisma is in a leader. If an authentic, consistent identity based on our personal strengths is key to succeeding, this is an extra challenge for women who may too often find themselves in a male-dominant culture they feel they need to fit into – and huge credit goes to the women who don't get pulled into this and stay authentic.[7]All these Super 7% women knew when they had landed in the right place (even if this was just luck, as one CEO told me it was in her case), or knew to get out of the wrong one. One COO said, 'I knew I wasn't comfortable in aggressive cultures, so I avoided them.' Anna Lawton, ex-Managing Director in an investment banking firm, realised early on that she did not belong in Trading and moved to Operations, which was the right place for her to leverage her strengths.

Robyn Johnstone, Group CEO of the Education Placement Group, experienced, a real 'Boys' Club' culture with sexist language everywhere early in her career – so she became proactive about getting into, and creating, cultures she liked. Robyn is also one of many of the women who stress the importance of working in a place with the right people in leadership. She's very aware of how lucky she was to later have a man like Julian Harley (now Chairman at AdviserPlus) as a boss and mentor who is a 'gentleman who always listens to people'. Hanneke Faber is extremely clear how important it was for her to have the support of the much-loved Paul Polman from early on in her career. Some may say these women were fortunate to land in the right place with the right people, but there is a lot more to it than that – these women had the self-awareness to know themselves, their strengths and where and with whom they could be successful as their authentic selves. I believe this is one of the key drivers behind the women who are winning at work.

However, what differentiates the Super 7% from the rest of women is not, of course, that they have been able to breeze through their lives and careers without facing any of the gender barriers or discomfort most women face. Just like the rest of us, they don't enjoy performances reviews; in the words of Patricia Rodríguez Barrios, Vice President of La Liga (the Spanish football league) and CEO of SmartBank Club, 'I didn't feel comfortable talking about myself, my achievements.' And many also dislike talking about their salary or requesting an increase; Tamara Ingram said, 'I feel awkward about even discussing it!', Hanneke Faber that Aris (her husband) 'forces me to', and Robyn Johnstone that 'I force myself to do it, but in writing.' In many cases, this is driven by a sense that they don't need more money (while most men would ask what that has to with anything!). Fama Francisco told me, 'I make more money than I ever imagined I could make' and Sylvie Moreau that 'I'm outrageously paid'. They have all also been ignored in meetings, been victims of the 'Hepeat' and been the only woman in the executive meeting. One COO joked:

> I work in the beauty business for God's sake and still find myself to be the only woman in some meetings!

Sylvie Moreau shared that she has failed to influence some important decisions in meetings because she had nobody there endorsing her point of view and Dame Cilla Snowball has experienced the same: 'Men believe they can override women... nobody came to my defence.' They have also missed out on promotions for no clear reason. One Super 7% woman told me she was once not on the (otherwise entirely male...) shortlist for the CEO role when she was as qualified as the other candidates. They have also felt a need to prove themselves before they are taken seriously. Patricia Rodríguez Barrios felt this acutely in the football world: 'I have to *show* them that I know, a man doesn't.' They have also faced overt and outrageous sexism. Patricia received a text from one of her male employees starting 'Hey baby'. And Anna Lawton of investment banking was told by a senior manager on becoming pregnant that 'You can't be a working mum on the trading floor' (where only ten of the 350 traders were women). Worse still, they have also been on the end of male bullying and sexual harassment. One sad reality is they felt that the last place to turn to for help was their HR department. So, they handled the issue indirectly to avoid career trouble for themselves (not surprising to me though, as, I have rarely seen HR support a woman's harassment complaint versus a senior man).

So, if these women have faced the same barriers most of us women have, what keeps them from being defeated by it all and giving up? They are all individuals but the one thing they have in common, though they display it in different ways, is enormous strength and resilience. Dame Cilla Snowball says, 'You build an inner steel that protects you' and believes this is something men build much earlier, even as schoolboys (which is ironic given that women need it more!). Doreen Bogdan-Martin shared:

> I think, looking back, that I've had staying power when others might have given up. I am determined, and when faced with obstacles my determination becomes stronger.

There is a courage and fearlessness in these women, a refusal to be beaten, not even by the bullies. Sylvie Moreau told me, 'I will push to the end' and Tamara Ingram said that 'The inner force is stronger than the barriers.' They are also living proof that women's competitiveness and ambition may not show up in the same way, but it is there; many of them talk about an inner force and acute desire to be the best at what they do. Sylvie Moreau is a self-professed 'Alpha-type' and says simply, 'I like winning'. Tamara Ingram told me:

> If I was a producer, I would want to be an Oscar-winning producer. If I was a teacher, I would want to be Head Teacher. On day one at Saatchi, I said I'm going to be CEO. I can't imagine being in something and not running it.

Fama Francisco has her own take on the same drive:

> I need to try to be the best to make it worth it. If I am
> going to do this in an average way, why am I doing it
> at all?

A key driver of this confidence and fearlessness is their shared
clarity that work (in most people's case) is not life or death,
it is ultimately a game and isn't to be taken personally or too
seriously. As Anna Lawton says in her own inimitable style,
'Fuck it, it's only work.' Hanneke Faber told me, 'I kind of
look at work like a game' and one CEO said that she 'learnt
not to take it personally'. I think this is one of those things
that will be obvious to many men out there reading this but
not so obvious to many women. We can learn a lot from the
women (and men) who accept the game and get on the pitch
and play it. As one female COO told me:

> I don't believe that decisions are made on the golf course.
> If I really believed that was the case, I would get a zero
> handicap. You need to get yourself in the game, not sit
> on the outside heckling. Solve from within, don't be a
> victim.

And she was not alone in having zero interest in being a victim
of the 'men versus women' dynamic. Fama Francisco remembers
that, even from a very early age as a young girl in the Philippines
(and sometimes to her mother's dismay), she 'always wanted to
do things even if they were not seen as something a girl would
do'.

Another thing these women have in common is their
attitude to perfectionism versus failure. While virtually all of
them admitted to being 'swotty' perfectionists at school and
at heart, they have had to learn not to be. They believe that
80/20 pragmatist/perfectionist is the only way to succeed in
the real world. Dame Cilla Snowball was told early on in

her career, 'Nobody likes a perfectionist, you're exhausting!' while Fama Francisca learnt to 'Focus on excellence not perfection.'

As for failure, it isn't a paralyser for them in the way it can be for many women. In part, this is again because they don't see work (and thus failing at it) as a matter of life and death, but also because they are able to rationalise failure – it's not personal, it's not a judgement upon them or their value. They are able to put failure very clearly into perspective. 'It's not the be all and end all, there's a much bigger world out there,' as Fama Francisco says and, in the words of Hanneke Faber, 'What are they going to do, fire me? I don't need more money; I'd find another job.' Easier, perhaps, for her to say now than for someone more junior and less well-paid, but all young women would do well to develop the confidence to know that one does not rely on one employer or job for life.

What we see here is that critical, and somewhat para-doxical, link between the acceptance of failure as an inevitable part of life and work and the confidence that comes with this – these women have, in Sylvie Moreau's words 'the opposite of imposter syndrome'. Patricia Rodríguez Barrios credits her parents for always giving her the confidence to try, that 'You are the best and you can do it but it is ok to fail, so what?' and, as a consequence, she has a deep sense of 'Trust in me' and is never afraid to put herself forward: 'I prefer to make a mistake and learn from it than not to try.'

There is no doubt that parents and upbringing played a key positive role in the development of many of these women. Doreen Bogdan-Martin shared that:

> The importance of equality is something I learnt from my parents. Both of them were absolutely committed to the principles of equality of opportunity.

A female COO acknowledged that coming from a working-class background and being the first person in her family to go to university was foundational for her, supported by her parents who always encouraged her. Tamara Ingram talks of learning, early in her life, that she absolutely must, without question, have financial independence. Robyn Johnstone also thanks her childhood for her strength and resilience – she was brought up on a cattle station in the outback of Australia as one of six children and was working and driving tractors from the age of eight.

Unsurprisingly, virtually all of these women told me that sport has always been an important part of their lives and something that built up their resilience. Hanneke Faber was a national champion high-diver from the age of 10 to 22 and she told me that, once you have done that, 'not much is going to scare you. What's the worst that can happen?' Diving taught her confidence, risk-taking and to have no fear and she draws a clear parallel between sport and work: 'Sport is about competitive performance, careers are about performing.' Robyn Johnstone has also always loved and played sport and says it made her 'not ashamed to be competitive', taught her about 'learning to deal with failure' and about the importance of being 'match fit for work'. A female COO also told me, 'I always loved sports' and that they have taught her relationship-building and how to develop a thick skin and hold her own with banter, saying, 'I feel more robust than most females.'

However, I believe that the two most important differentiators between the Super 7% women who win at work and the rest of us are how they manage men and childcare. All these women, without fail, have developed very clear techniques for managing their male colleagues and bosses. In the words of Patricia Rodríguez Barrios, 'You need strategies for handling men.' Most, if not all, of these women dislike and avoid open confrontation (Anna Lawton told me she learnt this from her academic parents who resolved all issues with calm discussion), and they manage conflict well if it arises and are never aggressive. They consider this to be a key part of professionalism and that to have a successful, sustainable career it is important to be liked or, at least, to 'not piss people off'. Doreen Bogdan-Martin told me, 'I have had to learn a lot of diplomatic skills'; Dame Cilla Snowball says, 'I don't want to make enemies'; and Robyn Johnstone sees it simply and pragmatically:

> Don't have fights if you don't need to, or if you're going to lose anyway.

These women are smart and know that nobody likes to look small or to lose and they have an acute awareness of the male ego and the need to manage it. As Sylvie Moreau says, 'Don't cut his balls off!'

One of their favourite shared strategies for managing men is over-preparation (some confess to this to an obsessive degree). For Doreen Bogdan-Martin, 'Being prepared, or even over-prepared' is key and Fama Francisco has a 'notebook of favourite go-to phrases' that she keeps in front of her for the difficult moments or challenging questions and always prepares for meetings by anticipating the concerns and disagreements that will come. The female TV presenter told me that for her it is about 'Above all calmness. And preparation. I game what they will say to me. And I work out exactly what the chess moves are… I am conscious of my tone, my calmness and a need to be logical and well prepared. I tend to keep emotion out of it, which is perhaps my way of acknowledging a male/female way of doing things.' For some of them, a key part of their preparation is to analyse the men they will be working or meeting with and develop a strategy based on this. Patricia Rodríguez Barrios says, 'I try to know the man in front of me.'

Another thing they all share is that they don't keep pushing if they aren't getting anywhere. Fama Francisco told me, 'I know when to disengage and go one on one' and Doreen Bogdan-Martin stressed that sometimes one needs to take a longer view, to recognise that you can lose a battle, but that persistence can eventually win the war.

Knowing how to fight another day, or another way is a common theme. Tamara Ingram recognised early on that, with her personality, she wouldn't win with some men and changed her approach accordingly, sometimes bringing other men on board to push the point through, sometimes even playing to their egos and making herself seem less senior (or subservient, even) in order to get the result. Whatever strategies these women use, they all know that they need them, that this is a game like any other that needs to be analysed and prepared for, a performance that needs to be delivered – that just turning up and 'being yourself' with no preparation is not going to cut it. Knowing this and actioning it in a way that is authentic is the challenge, and maybe the ability to do this is one big differentiating skill these successful women have. Fama Francisco puts it well:

It's too purist to say I am who I am. You have to adjust – but to be more effective, not to change who you are.

One of the clearest strategies that all of these women spontaneously spoke of leveraging is a sense of humour, including partaking in banter and a liberal use of sarcasm. They all see this as probably the most effective tool to manage conflict with men and are aware of this important skill. The TV presenter described one of her key strengths as being 'very funny' and this as being key to her ability to be forthright with a non-threatening tone. Doreen Bogdan-Martin is also clear on its important role:

Making the point with firmness and sometimes even some ironic humour can often be more effective than a confrontational approach.

Anna Lawton told me, 'I don't like conflict and my first defence mechanism is humour and sarcasm.' She isn't afraid to dish it out to men either, often using the lines, 'Well who's behaving like an archetypal trading bastard?' or 'Oh we are getting on our high horse aren't we?' and told me one of her early insights about the men in her working world of trading was that 'They all respond to the school ma'am.' Anna also admitted to leveraging the power of 'deliberate excessive swearing' when needed! These women have all understood that there are some things that a lot of men profoundly respect and a great sense of humour and ability to hold one's own in the midst of the fray is one of them. I certainly felt this respect from the men I interviewed for this book. Julian Harley said it was one of the things he likes most about the way Robyn Johnstone manages and communicates with him, even in stressful situations. 'A good sense of humour' was one of the top things cited as a key positive in Fama Francisco by the many men who see her as the strongest female leader they have come across in P&G.

When you think about it, isn't it obvious that humour is so powerful? First and foremost, it is a big sign that someone is relaxed and confident in themselves if they can step back and have a laugh about something (and we know how much we value confidence in people). Secondly, when we are laughing with someone, we're friends, we're on the same side, we're not fighting with or confronting each other – and everyone responds positively to this. It's interesting that, when I asked Doreen Bogdan-Martin what she believes has differentiated her from other, less successful women, one of her key thoughts was, 'I've never seen my male colleagues as the enemy.' I would bet many highly successful women would share this view and that they have demonstrated this by managing situations with humour, not aggression and conflict – and that this is also felt and understood by their male colleagues and is one of the reasons they are admired as leaders by them.

We have seen how important upbringing was in fostering

confidence in the Super 7% and, as one successful woman after another told me about her strategies for handling men, it emerged that most of them had also learnt this in their childhood from their early interactions with their fathers.

In their own different ways, they learnt that there was no need to fear men or they learnt how to manage them in order to avoid their anger. At the positive end of the spectrum, Sylvie Moreau's father was a small, never-threatening man with a gentle voice and her mum was the strong, angry one – this taught her as a child that men were not to be feared and it was natural and safe for a woman to stand up to them (although of course not every young girl has this experience).

At a more sinister point on the spectrum, we have the female CMO who, when asked if she ever feels a slight sense of fear of men at work, for example when discussions get heated, she clearly found this a slightly bizarre question and said, 'Er, no.' As we went on to talk about why this was and where her fearlessness came from, it emerged that as a child her father resorted to hitting her when he was pushed or angry and she eventually came to realise that 'This was all he had'; if the worst that can happen is a man losing his temper and lashing out then there is no reason to be fearful. As a result, she is not one of the women who is afraid of men and of pushing her arguments as far as she needs to. We also have the CEO with the military father who may have, I speculate, contributed to her aggressive, tough, masculine style.

Then we have the example of Robyn Johnstone, who grew up with a bad-tempered father who the whole family feared. But Robyn worked out how to handle him to avoid things reaching conflict point and from that experience she 'learnt to deal with difficult men'.

This was one of the biggest insights into the way successful women manage themselves and manage men – and I could feel that it was somewhat of an epiphany for these women as well. As they were talking through it, they realised where it began and how their interactions with men from childhood taught them to behave as fully grown women in the boardroom. A lack of fear of men, or 'managing around' conflict to avoid the fear is something all of these women have in common. That this should be an important driver of their success makes sense – I believe so many women are afraid at some level of men and it ultimately makes them stop pushing and back down. In doing this, they send a signal that they don't have sufficient confidence in themselves and in what they are saying – and this is the opposite of what strong leaders do. In Doreen Bogdan-Martin's words:

> Timidity simply doesn't pay off in the work environment. Many cultures teach women to be meek and self-effacing. This really isn't going to work in most corporate roles.

Courage is key to leadership; fearlessness is hugely admired in leaders. The women who don't feel (or show) fear have a very big advantage over the ones who do.

One of the things all of the Super 7% were united on was that women must try to keep control of their emotions and avoid crying publicly in the workplace. Tamara Ingram said simply, 'You just can't do it' and Sylvie Moreau that 'Composure is a better trait'. Hanneke Faber shared that, in difficult meetings, she has seen other women red-faced and tearful and known, regretfully, that this was doing them no favours in the eyes of their male colleagues. Ex-British Prime Minister Theresa May clearly saw this the same way; in response to an overwhelming defeat in January 2019 she showed no emotion, no anger (it is said not even when behind closed doors where she shrugged it off with simply 'it's politics'). And when she did finally show some emotion upon her resignation, she was heavily criticised for it. A senior P&G manager once summarised it as 'To succeed as a woman in a man's world, you need to learn to share your emotions, unemotionally.'

Interestingly, these other women take this clear 'No tears'

stance despite being very much seen and appreciated as 'Authentic Women' and knowing that the urge and need to cry is very natural and real for women. One told me that being your authentic self is not the same as allowing your natural self to run free at all times, that authenticity doesn't mean lack of any control. And perhaps one day, when we live in an equal and more inclusive, diverse world, there will be more acceptance of emotion as part and parcel of being a human being (woman or man).

So the Super 7%'s first key differentiator is their strategies for managing men; the second is that not a single one of them has had to carry the majority of the burden for looking after their home or children. Many of them laid out the simple reality that, to get to the top, you have to put in more hours and be more committed than other people. Tamara Ingram said, 'It's not 9 to 5.' Across the world women carry 80% plus of the housework and childcare so it's challenging to have the capacity for doing a big, senior job – well, these women do have the capacity.[8] Two of the Super 7% I spoke with don't need to worry about the burden at all because they don't have kids and they acknowledged how much easier this made it for them, including being 'able to go the extra yard, at weekends, or to travel'. In Patricia Rodríguez Barrios' words, 'I have no kids to manage'. For the others, they have had a lot of help. Fama Francisco shared that her husband has always taken on 'genuinely half' of managing the home and family. Hanneke Faber also shared the importance of 'a very supportive home front'. Thanks to her husband Aris and paid help she has never managed more than 50% of the childcare or 25% of the household. One CEO also used the phrase 'supportive home front' and told me her husband has always done more than half of the work at home: 'I'm married to someone who is very supportive of my career.' Doreen Bogdan-Martin has four kids, of which three are triplets, and she cites the necessity of 'reliable and trustworthy home help'. Robyn Johnstone recognises that she couldn't have done it without a full-time nanny (which many cannot afford), or her husband, who has worked for most of their marriage, picking up the slack and taking time off when needed. Tamara Ingram told me her husband 'was COO of the house' and 'incredibly hands-on.' Anna Lawton's husband has never worked and has done 90% of the work in bringing up their three kids, only once calling her at work to say she needed to come home because one of them was in hospital. She says that, thanks to him, her bosses did not feel the need to put her on 'the mommy track' and that

> there is absolutely no way I could have been this
> successful if Mark hadn't given up work.

She also points out how important it is not just that he took this on, but also that he was 'not emasculated' by it. Sylvie Moreau also talks about her working yet supportive husband. These women are lucky to have this kind of support; in Dame Cilla Snowball's words, 'Top women have a supportive man, or no man at all.'

Another thing these women all have in common (and I really hate to say this) is their attitude to how to dress in the workplace. Tamara Ingram told me, 'I had to learn how to dress, that work comes with a uniform' and she was by no means the only one to say that there is a 'work wardrobe', you have to 'look the part'. Dame Cilla Snowball goes further and describes it as 'armour'. Hanneke Faber says, 'I do believe the way women dress affects how they are perceived.' For Patricia Rodríguez Barrios, it is a tool she uses to make a virtue out of being the only woman in the male-dominated football environment: 'I try to be the different person, to wear a different colour and stand out.' For one COO, how women dress at work is a big passion area. We had run out of time in our interview and I had not been able to ask her views on it, but she spontaneously shared them: 'I understand the male locker-room psyche, they will talk about your bum, not your work.' It is something she says she has always coached young women on and continues to do so when she sees them dressing in a certain 'non-uniform' way, telling them to not 'make it a topic of conversation.'

It is a highly controversial area I know, advising women on how to dress in order to manage around the sex-based thoughts and comments of men. It is also true that dressing professionally and 'appropriately' will not always be enough to stop the sexist comments, if a woman's shapely figure is still discernible for example. But it is fair to say that a work uniform is not just for women. Men clearly have one too, although for different reasons. How many men do we think would prefer not to wear a suit, or a shirt and tailored trousers? I'm sure they would like to put on their jeans, trackies or shorts but they don't.

Now as someone who has always believed in being myself and wearing, doing and saying what I want, I find it a little difficult to accept that some of these things are important drivers of the success of these amazing women. I personally prefer Eleanor Roosevelt's philosophy that 'Well-behaved women rarely make history' but the reality is that, to an extent, these highly successful women are being 'well-behaved', and they are the ones making history by reaching the top levels in their chosen careers when, frankly, most women are not. They are authentic women but that doesn't mean they are always showing up *au naturel* – they are thinking and acting strategically in the way they dress, in the way they prepare, in the way they analyse the people they are working with and how to manage them to get the result they want. What we perhaps need to remember here is that this isn't a gender thing, this is something that only women have to do in order to succeed – men are thinking about and doing all of this too.

One thing these highly successful women also do very well, consistent with many women, is working with and managing people. They virtually all talk about how much they love and value people, and they know that relationships are very important. Anna Lawton speaks of her 'genuine interest in the other point of view' and being 'genuinely interested in people'.

Tamara Ingram, too, told me, 'I've always liked people, from being a child. I'm interested in their motivations and the whole person. I don't mind the bad bits. I've not made it because I'm more intelligent or talented, it's because I care about people and I take them with me.'

They all understand the fundamental pillar of Jim Collins' level 5 Leadership concept, which is to focus on other people and not on the self.[9] They know what Channel 4's Zaid Al-Qassab believes to be the most important leadership insight there is: 'Business is achieved by human beings, they are the asset.' Fama Francisco describes herself as 'a genuine human being who cares' and believes that, 'Your success is determined by how many people want to follow you with their heart.' These are not just her words about herself; one of her senior male employees talks of her 'incredible ability to keep people engaged and energised.' Dame Cilla Snowball is also a clear 'people person' who told me how much she 'enjoys clients' and her love of and care for people is very much noticed and appreciated by others, including men. Sal Pajwani says she is 'the most empathetic person I know, in a conversation with you she is 150% in your world' and Zaid Al-Qassab describes her as

> a parent, a supporter to her people, serving others above all else. She really cares for her people 100% of the time, for their wellbeing and development.

It's no surprise then that these women have succeeded, and succeeded in a way that is highly admired and respected by those who have worked with and for them. Clifton and Harter found that

> managers who create environments in which employees can make the most of their talents have more productive work units with less employee turnover.[10]

Indeed, as Mervyn Davies said:

> The litmus test of a great leader is whether they can quickly write down on a piece of paper all of the people they have developed.[11]

I would bet a lot of money that these women can.

What is inspiring for me is that this isn't something that women have had to integrate or copy or perform or strategise about, this is something that seems to come more naturally to women in general and many of the Super 7% are embracing that and leveraging it to bring them success as leaders. While there is not as much of a gender skew as I would have expected in some strengths, with women and men sharing four of five of the top CliftonStrengths® themes (Responsibility®, Input®, Learner®, Relator®), there are some differences.[12] For women, it is Empathy® that rounds out the top 5 (versus Achiever® for men) and women also rank higher than men do on the Developer®, Discipline® and Includer® themes. They are more likely to focus on planning, routine and structure (Discipline®), more apt to accept, include and build loyalty with others (Includer® and Empathy®) and have a higher propensity for recognising and cultivating the potential in people (Developer®). Women get and give energy through collaboration and are generally more inclined to focus on groups or teams and cultivating relationships, perhaps explaining why – as managers – they lead more engaged teams.[13] Empathy® and Developer® in particular are key level 5 Leadership strengths and in leveraging diversity (ironic that we need women to leverage the diversity of women). So, these are people skills that women are generally stronger in, but many are lost in male-dominated cultures overflowing with gender barriers that make them feel they need to copy the behaviours and strengths of others rather than using their own 'feminine power'.[14] Perhaps the biggest and simplest secret of all behind the success of these women is simply – bring yourself.

One other piece of good news from this is that the majority of the Super 7% women I talked with were big champions of other women. Hanneke Faber promoted women disproportionately when she was at Ahold, resulting in half of her General Managers being women. Sylvie Moreau always speaks of 'the sisterhood'; 40% of her Lead Team are women and her mantra is 'to inspire my sisters in the workplace'. Fama Francisco says:

> I'm intentional about finding hidden gem women early on in their career and getting them into the right job.

She believes her 'personal principles should show up in the composition of my Lead Team', so ensures she has a 50/50 mix. She believes that for young career women, her 'role is giving them hope [that] somebody like me can succeed'. Doreen Bogdan-Martin led the creation of ITU's first gender task force and Patricia Rodríguez Barrios leads a mentoring programme for women in Spain. Robyn Johnstone does a lot of work reassuring women that they can have children and a career, and backs this up concretely by giving them work flexibility (which she does for men too, by the way). Tamara Ingram is happy to describe herself as an 'absolute feminist' and Dame Cilla Snowball is passionate on the gender equality front and one of the women who likes to 'bang on about it… I can hear the eye-rolling'. Happily, these women are not alone – whatever we think of her time in leadership, Theresa May is the first female British Prime Minister to call herself a feminist. She consistently promoted women in government (Margaret Thatcher famously did not believe in 'women's lib' and pulled up the ladder behind her) and said that she wouldn't be the last female Prime Minister. This is heartening indeed and let's hope we see more of this in the future from more women at the top. If we want more women to win at work, we need the ones who are succeeding to help, teach and support the others because, as we have seen, it's far from easy and there is a huge amount to learn.

In so many ways, these Super 7% are exceptional women and I have huge admiration for them. They are not just highly intelligent and competent, they are also very self-aware people who know themselves and where and how they need to work in order to succeed as their authentic selves, who know and leverage their strengths, and who aren't just clever but are savvy about people (and specifically men) and how to work with them in a way that gets the best out of everyone. They are strong, resilient and courageous, and not afraid to stand up for what they believe in or to try things even if they may fail. They don't take work personally and they are willing to work extremely long hours and be away from home and family (to an extent which some women, and men, may never be in order to 'win'). If this is the bar for women to win at work, it is a high one. We can admire and learn from the Super 7% but the reality today is they are a little like a rare species of animal. If the 7% is going to become more like 50%, men are also going to need to help lower the bar which today is higher than it should be.

Sisters are (not) doing it for themselves

WOMEN TALK A lot about 'sisterhood'. But, I'm afraid to say that, in a career of 27 years so far, and setting aside what I heard from the Super 7% women, I haven't seen much evidence of a sisterhood in the workplace. We know how important it is that women reach senior levels and help others emulate their success. Women need *female* mentors to succeed – Boris Groysberg, a professor at Harvard Business School, conducted a study of 1,000 women stock analysts and found that most women who had risen to high levels had mentors, and that

> men who do mentor women can't offer much in the way
> of psychological support – how to deal with sexism, for
> instance, or how to balance a career and family.[1]

However, despite this, many women tell me that they don't believe that having women at the top would lead to more women following in their footsteps. Several women say that the worst and most demotivating boss they ever had was a woman. And what is pretty humiliating for women is that men see this lack of support (and, worse, even animosity) they comment on it, saying that women are 'too busy bickering' to get things done and 'too jealous and threatened' to support each other.

I don't just think this is sad and embarrassing, I believe it's another one of the important reasons men win at work and women don't. Men are out there supporting and promoting their male mini-mes, but not enough women are doing the same for other women. Sisterhood this is not. Even when we get a few women up there in the top jobs we don't leverage this to help more women up the ladder and move us towards a more equal gender split. In too many cases the women up there succeeding aren't supporting other women. Well shame on us ladies. As Madeline Albright, the first woman to become the US Secretary of State, said, 'There's a special place in hell for women who don't help other women.'[2]

So why aren't more women supporting other women and helping them to succeed?

We have seen that some women have feminist phobia and just don't want to be associated with the gender cause, believing it makes them seem weak. They prefer to 'rise above' these issues for fear of being seen as part of them, for fear it will be assumed that they are speaking personally on behalf of themselves rather than for gender equality generally. For me, this is tantamount to not wanting to be associated with women and not being proud of and wanting to be seen as a woman – they prefer to be seen as 'one of the boys' because it is safer. In my view any woman who feels and acts like this is not just not supporting other women; she is betraying them and herself. I say shame on you if you have been lucky to make it into a great position as a woman and you are not acknowledging your fortune and leveraging your success and position to help others.

One theory of mine is that there is a lack of sisterhood because successful women are more rare than successful men. and these women have therefore always been used to being the 'Queen Bee' or the 'special woman' in a male-dominant group. As long as they can remember, they were probably always the one who was the strong and confident woman. Perhaps they feel threatened when they encounter another 'special woman' on their team. They are used to competing and working with men but less so with other women; maybe at some level they don't want to see the other woman be or become as 'special' as she is (or, potentially, even more successful and special). It's also possible that competition is less healthy amongst women because of the scarcity of senior roles for women, whereas men see senior men everywhere and thus feel more of a sense of abundance of success. When we are part of a successful group, we can be pleased for and even proud of each other – but when we see someone else rising and succeeding within the context of scarcity, we will naturally respond less positively and even with envy and fear.

Another hypothesis is that this unhealthy competitiveness between women again comes back to our beginnings and, to extent, our reproductive biology. We know that the original biological mission of the males of a species is to 'spread their seed' as far and wide as possible, impregnating every female and creating as many babies as they could in order for their species to survive and flourish. Meanwhile, the priority of the female of the species is to ensure that their baby is kept safe and healthy, so it could also go on one day to continue the cycle of generating and contributing more babies towards the species. In order to do this, the female needed to create a nest and ensure there was food for the baby. For this she needed a male – who was of course hard to pin down as his natural driving force was to be off spreading his seed somewhere. And so, the female was originally programmed to work hard to compete for and win the strongest, best man and then keep him away from the other females, who were her competition in her important role as mother and contributor to the species. Competition is of course a key dynamic here for both males and females, but again the scarcity mindset created by the female mission potentially leads to a more defensive, jealous instinct. Perhaps women have at some level retained this sentiment towards other women as competition when they are in the context of men and this is what we now sometimes see manifesting itself in the workplace when they see a woman be superior to them or to get into a position which they feel threatens their own.

Now I really shudder at this theory, as I'm sure most women do, but if I am honest, I have seen women behave in this demeaning, competitive and even bitchy way towards each other too many times to discount that there is something going on under the surface here. I have seen it at work (have been on the wrong end of it from more than one female boss in fact) and I have seen it perhaps most visibly in sport. I am an enormous fan of netball – I played it for nearly 40 years and work to promote it as a perfect way to keep girls in sport (more on this later), so it pains me to see some of the behaviour I have sometimes seen from women behind the scenes of the game. Over the years and various occasions I have heard comments made and seen emails written between women organising tournaments (which are supposed to be a fun and enjoyable thing), criticising other women sometimes quite personally for 'always behaving this way', or saying 'I don't know who she thinks she is.'

I truly hate to hear and see this stuff happening between women but I have, sadly, seen it way too often to bury it beneath the carpet and pretend it doesn't occur – and I must admit that, when it does, it certainly does look like it is a form of competitiveness and jealousy and an attempt to ensure that no woman is allowed to 'get above herself', or certainly not to be seen to be 'better than me'. I have asked myself whether this kind of thing happens when boys and men get together on a Saturday for a football tournament and, frankly, I don't believe for a second that it does. Most men just don't behave this way towards each other. They just want to have some fun, get some exercise and have a beer and a chat about it afterwards – and if something goes wrong, they might have a quick go at someone, probably with some humour and banter, and then it's over with. It's no wonder more teenage boys than girls keep playing and enjoying sport. And it's no wonder we women don't have a sisterhood in the high-stakes context of work and career if we can't even manage to have one when we're organising a fun weekend sport event.

Another theory is that a woman's generally lower level of confidence affects their ability to be in 'healthy' competition with another in the way that men do (especially if it's fragile). Does it erode women's confidence to see other women being strong and talented and seeming confident? Does it make them feel better to criticise other women in order to bring them down and re-level things? Does the generally higher level of confidence that we see in men mean that they don't feel such a sense of jealousy and don't feel the need to put other men down? We know that men can be highly competitive for all the reasons discussed, but perhaps their competitiveness manifests itself in a different way that is grounded in self-confidence and therefore more direct and healthier than the female version.

These are the best hypotheses I have on why women are not supporting and promoting each other in the way that men do. But what I know for sure is that women need to get over whatever it is that drives this and start looking after their sisters, because men are certainly looking after their brothers. If we keep on this way, I think we can see which gender is going to keep winning at work and getting the best jobs. This Pinterest post seems a good way to close this chapter: 'A strong woman stands up for herself. A stronger woman stands up for others!' There are many reasons for gender imbalance that we can pin on men but this one is entirely on us to fix ladies – and shame on us if we don't.

12

The cruel bit

WE HAVE SEEN many reasons why men win at work, but the really cruel thing in all of this for women is that, even if they understand these reasons and try to re-apply and copy them, they still cannot win. That's because what works for men doesn't necessarily work for women and women who try to do the things that men do are often criticised and disliked. So, this is the cruel bit ladies – there is a 'male way' of operating that leads to salary increases and advancement; but if a woman tries to adopt it, she may be disliked and penalised. Author Dr Halee Gray Scott sums it up this way:

> To succeed, you need to be liked, but to be liked, you
> need to temper your success.[1]

As we have previously shown, women don't always like to see other women succeed. As the two women find in *Tall Poppies*, the trouble with being a tall poppy is people will try to cut you down to size.[2] And we all know how some stay-at-home mums bitch about the career women – how many times have we heard a woman say 'what's the point in having children if you're never going to be around to look after them?'

Alexandra Burke, in *Strictly Come Dancing* in 2017, was the perfect example of a 'tall poppy'. Despite being an absolutely brilliant dancer and getting top scores from the judges, Alexandra Burke was in the bottom two acts for two consecutive weeks – and was the victim of a lot of nasty comments in the media. And, when it came to the final, there were three fantastic women and one man and, guess what, the man won. Now the winner, Joe McFadden, seems like a very nice man and his dancing improved enormously during the course of the competition but I think anyone could see that Alexandra Burke was in a totally different class. Sadly, she learnt the hard way that being excellent at something as a woman is not necessarily going to make you popular, especially with other women (*Strictly Come Dancing* voting is one of the few things in life that is female-dominated![3]). As Professor Iris Bohnet tells us:

> Dozens of studies have now demonstrated that women face a trade-off between competence and likeability.[4]

We cannot avoid the reality that being liked (or at least not disliked) is an important consideration for women. In 2015, the actress Jennifer Lawrence talked about why she had allowed herself to be under-paid versus her male co-stars for a leading role in *American Hustle*:

> I would be lying if I didn't say that there was an element of wanting to be liked that influenced my decision to close the deal without a fight. I didn't want to seem difficult or spoiled.[5]

Perhaps this fear of being disliked is another remnant from the beginning of society, when we couldn't take the risk of unpopularity within our community of women for our own protection and survival. Wherever it comes from, it seems to be very much present in the psyche of women.

We have talked about the real and significant salary gap between men and women, and about women being a lot less likely to discuss or request a pay increase – and even when they do, they are less likely to receive one or will get a lower one than a man would. But do you know what's even more cruel than this? Research has shown that people accept men asking for salary increases but do not like it when women ask for better remuneration because this violates gender norms, so people prefer female employees who don't ask.[6] In a similar vein, an experiment was done on employees' wage demands at the point of hiring. It had no effect on how men were perceived but was perceived negatively in women. So, women really can't win – they don't get equal pay because they don't ask, but when they do ask they don't get it anyway and they are disliked for having asked (perhaps at some level women sense this and that's why they don't ask!). It also doesn't work for women when they rise above their belief in the 'myth of meritocracy' and attempt to put themselves forward for a job – a Lean In/McKinsey survey in 2016 of 34,000 employees found that women who negotiated for promotions were 30% more likely than men to be seen as intimidating, bossy or aggressive.[7]

Women can't win when it comes to deciding how to dress either. If she in any way displays any evidence that she is, in fact, an actual woman with an actual woman's body parts then she is seen as 'too feminine' and not taken seriously. Sarah Palin was described as 'Too Sexy for the White House'[8] and the *Washington Post* commented on Hillary Clinton's 'undeniable cleavage' in a photo where less than half a centimetre of 'cleavage' was visible.[9]

A male lawyer I know told me about the 'Power Skirt', which is apparently an in-joke amongst his male colleagues that they share when an attractive female in a short, fitted skirt is brought along to a meeting, the understanding being that she is there purely to distract the opposition rather than having any intelligence or insight to add to the discussion.

As a woman, this stuff sends shivers down my spine. It makes me simultaneously feel the need to only wear polo-necks for every future business interaction with men and extremely angry that men should be able to make us feel this way. And of course, women can't win because if we did adopt the polo-neck strategy, we would be seen as not feminine enough. This may be a successful strategy from a career development point of view (*Forbes* magazine believes that Angela Merkel's 'frumpy style... proved an asset to her career'[10]) but most women I know don't want to be seen as unfeminine and 'manly' – they want to be allowed to be a woman and for this not to be negative or career-limiting. That doesn't seem to me to be too much to ask.

And another thing. Remember we discussed the importance of speaking up in meetings as something we all unconsciously value as a 'sign of leadership', and something that it is proven women are less likely to do and less frequently than men? Well guess what, when women do this, it isn't received positively. Victoria Brescoll at Yale University found that male executives who spoke up in discussions were given higher ratings of competence and, yes it's true, the female executives who spoke up got lower competence ratings (from men and women by the way!).[11]

I suspect that the confidence factor is also playing a role here again and the women who spoke up didn't do so with the level of self-assurance of the men. The confidence versus competence equation is also likely to be at play – we forgive low content in confident men much more than we forgive over or under confidence in women (no matter how strong their competence and content is). It seems that when it comes to men and women and content worth listening to:

One has it until they lose it, while the other doesn't have it until they prove it.[12]

There is no doubt that speaking up in meetings is a sign of assertiveness and has been shown to be disliked as a trait in women. How often have you heard a woman being called (or even called her yourself) bossy, emotional or pushy or 'painful'? Theresa May was described by colleague Ken Clarke as 'a bloody difficult woman' and I for one have been called all of these things. Laura Bates notes the same phenomenon: 'assertiveness mysteriously becomes shrillness and tenacity morphs into nagging or hysteria.'[13] These are all negative words associated with dislike and we simply don't hear them used to describe men. The same traits would be described with positive, admiring words such as passionate, in control, assertive or tenacious.

People are also uneasy with women who seek power. I think Hillary Clinton is a great example of this – it seems she was always popular in the roles that she got and considered to be doing a very good job but was always disliked when she was at the stage of putting herself forward as the candidate for them. Research conducted after her loss in the presidential election has shown that it is hard for assertive, ambitious women to be seen as likeable and therefore are perceived as missing some intangible leadership quality.[14] It seems that men, unfortunately, don't always like to see too much strength in women and prefer to see us behaving in a gentler way. One of my great friends has really gained in confidence since first joining her company a few years ago but often her male colleagues tell her sadly that she used to be really nice, sweet and smiley. I remember one young HR manager telling me she had been told she should smile by one of the men in the audience during an important presentation she was giving about significant and difficult role eliminations. And a question to the women out there reading this – how many times in your life have you been told to smile or 'cheer up' when you're walking down the street? And the men…? Thought so.

Oh, and heaven forbid that a woman should go as far as to actually express anger in the workplace (because it's not as if there's anything there for us to get angry about, eh?). Victoria Brescoll also found that an angry man's salary is over 50% more than an angry woman's:

> When women express anger at work… they can be
> seen as out of control… it is almost expected for men
> to get angry… a man who gets irate at work may well
> be admired for it.[15]

So, a woman is 'too assertive if she gets angry and too weak if she cries.'[16] As a result, what we see is that women live in a constant state of trying to avoid being labelled 'difficult' or 'whining'. We have been taught from childhood that men like women who smile, and they don't like women who are wearisome. But if women just smile sweetly and don't show strength, we are never going to get important things said and done – and if women are strong and difficult, we're going to be disliked. Ultimately, neither option is going to make us successful then. Cruel.

Sarah Cooper has a lot of tongue-in-cheek advice for us on how to manage this cruel reality and no-win situation in *How to Be Successful Without Hurting Men's Feelings*:[17]

> Be vigilant about hiding yourself. (Not your entire self, just the woman… part of yourself.)… Scale the heights of your career and break that glass ceiling, but do it very quietly and gingerly… We have to be friendly, but not too friendly; awesome, but not too awesome; and completely comfortable in our own skin as long as we fit right in… Gender-neutralise your CV. Make sure your CV doesn't scream 'female'… Use initials instead of your full first name… Avoid all pronouns… Replace your picture… One great way to remove the sting of being a powerful woman is to give yourself a cute, feminine title that reminds investors that yes, you are a leader, but you are also still a woman (eg Mumpreneur)… Wedding ring: take it off – This will help you achieve that 'I won't be getting pregnant soon look'… Smile: not too flirty, not too bitchy… Hairstyle: not too sexy, not too boring… Voice: not too loud (very threatening), not too soft (lacking confidence)… Voice pitch is very tricky for women. Our normal speaking voices are naturally shrill and annoying, or too deep and not feminine enough. We must practise constantly to speak in a tone that's pleasing to the male ear. In fact,

we may be practising for the rest of our lives because this tone has not yet been discovered... If you don't take enough credit you won't seem qualified, but if you take too much credit, you'll seem arrogant... Salary: when asking to negotiate you might come off as demanding. But if you don't negotiate, people will think you don't value yourself... It's all about finding that perfect balance that doesn't exist.

Much as all this made me laugh out loud when I read her book, it is based on a dark truth that, in reality, is not funny at all. Every day we hear that we are 'too something' – we are too bossy, too aggressive, too assertive, too emotional – the word that tells us we have stepped out of the expected female role and is an attempt (that often succeeds) to control us, to tell us this is a bad thing and to make us withdraw. In her article 'Bloody Difficult Women', Sarra Manning (author of *The Rise and Fall of Becky Sharp*, the modern day version of *Vanity Fair*) puts it brilliantly:

It seems to me that whenever there's a woman living her best life, there'll always be a man telling her that she's too much. That, in fact, it would be best if she were a little less. But filing down the parts of yourself that others find disagreeable means that, in the end, you lose sight of who you are and who you could be. It's much better to have a reputation for being difficult than to spend life dancing to the beat of someone else's drum.[18]

'Likeability is not a rent that women should have to pay to take up space in the world'. Chimamanda Ngozi Adichie has a similar message in her plea for how we should raise a daughter:

Teach her to reject likeability. Her job is not to make herself likeable, her job is to be her full self... Show her

that she does not need to be liked by everyone. Tell her that
if someone doesn't like her, there will be someone else who
will. Teach her that she is not merely an object to be liked
or disliked, she is also a subject who can like and dislike.[19]

It is not an easy request of women though, to ask them, or
anyone in fact, not to care about likeability – it is surely a
fundamental human driver. The key issue here for me is that
women *are* sometimes disliked for exhibiting traits that are
considered completely normal, admirable even, in a man. The
answer is not for women to train themselves to stop caring
about their likeability, but for us to get ourselves used to seeing
women behaving in this way. This means we need to see more
women doing the senior leadership jobs, so this becomes a
normal thing for a woman to be doing and to be seen doing,
in the way it feels normal to see her carrying a baby. We stop
seeing her as unlikeable and describing her as bossy, pushy or
too manly and start thinking of her as a leader. So we need
to strive for gender equality in roles not just because this will
make business and society stronger but also because we need to
create a new, positive self-fulfilling prophecy.

Today's self-fulfilling prophecy is that the few women
who do make it to a senior level find it difficult to succeed
because there aren't enough of them to make them seem like
'normal', recognisable leaders to be liked and admired, rather
than outliers worthy of disdain and criticism. We need more
women in higher roles so we can all learn and get comfortable
with what a female leader looks like and behaves like. We
need women in their natural state to be recognised and
respected as leaders. Just as a man would be.

So why do men win at work?

MEN DON'T WIN at work because they are an evil force that is consciously trying to hold women back and prevent them from succeeding so they can keep all the good jobs and money for themselves. So, why do they win at work? In most cases, the reasons are unwitting, unconscious and even invisible. As a society we are still either in denial that gender inequality is a big issue, or we are diminishing its importance, or deflecting the discussion to other issues. There are even women who are denying it as an issue and undermining women who are trying to fight it. Too many of us have 'feminist phobia'.

Most men, thankfully, can disassociate themselves from the #MeToo predators and the bottom of the pyramid issues they would never contribute to – and some feel this means they can avoid engaging with other underlying gender inequality issues that every man contributes to (including good, well-intentioned men).

Gender inequality persists as a self-fulfilling prophecy due to the tiny percentage of female role models and representation we have in key positions and in the media. While we know the data shows that gender diversity is a win for everyone (men and women) that strengthens businesses, organisations and society and makes our lives better, we haven't really internalised and embraced this, and we don't make it a real priority. A McKinsey survey showed that only 40% of senior partners and 25% of managers considered diversity a priority[1] – isn't it interesting that leaders are so curious and probing on most other business issues but not on gender inequality, which is probably the biggest opportunity for growth they have? Even where we see some efforts in this area, in Helena Morrissey's words, 'diversity and inclusion are usually treated as enhancements, not as core to business success'.[2] Also, for many unconscious reasons, men think that men are better – because they are like them and like is comfortable with like. Given men have most of the top jobs and thus most of the hiring and promotion decisions, this becomes another self-fulfilling prophecy.

Then there is the invisible power of culture, where the members of the dominant group (white men, in most workplaces) are able to feel included and belonging, and to be relaxed, confident and authentic, and thus perform. Meanwhile, the non-dominant group (women) feel they don't belong and are excluded, don't feel comfortable and confident and don't therefore perform at their best, and often feel they need to try to 'fit in' and in doing so compromise their authenticity. And so the (dominant) men seem like stronger, better performers. In addition, the presence of men (which is often dominant) further undermines women's confidence and performance.

We all bring our unconscious bias to the workplace, which favours men over women – and without us realising it, this directs our opinions, decisions and actions to the detriment of women. There are also some biological differences between men and women that impact on their reactions to stress, conflict, risk-taking, power and hierarchy, aggressive competition, external feedback and also their lack of confidence, their sensitivity, emotional responses and need for connection and collaboration which can lead to men being seen as 'stronger'.

And of course, because men *are* undeniably generally stronger in the physical sense – which instils a subconscious fear of men in some women. This can affect how a woman reacts and the extent to which she is willing to push instead of withdrawing her opinions versus the extent to which a man is willing to (and thus demonstrate courageous leadership behaviour).

One key driver is when superior male confidence is confused

with superior competence and testosterone-driven 'gravitas' and communication style is seen as leadership. The clearest example is that men know how to 'give good meeting' – they are seen as stronger performers compared with the women who are talking less, more quietly and being interrupted before they can contribute their points. They are seen as stronger leaders.

Meanwhile, too many women believe in the myth of meritocracy, that life works like school and that getting 'A grades' is enough – while men know that this is a ridiculous concept in the reality of the workplace. Men understand what drives success at work, that competence and doing a good job is just 'table stakes' and that you need to also invest in networking, relationship-building with sponsors and self-marketing to ensure you are noticed 'under the umbrella' and ahead in the vote for roles and promotions. Men are also more comfortable discussing and negotiating salary, so they are paid (sometimes significantly) more. We are waiting for women to 'be like men' and be as comfortable with self-marketing, self-promotion, networking and salary negotiations. And in the meantime, we keep rewarding the men ahead of the women.

And we are expecting women to do all of these things and a good job, on top of carrying the lion's share of household work and childcare – and not realising that this causes women stress, exhaustion, illness and, in some cases, to decide to give up on their careers.

Men generally have more time to network, because they are carrying less of the household work and childcare burden. Seeing the men get the big jobs and the promotions and the bigger salary ahead of them makes women feel frustrated and not valued. And sometimes it leads to them giving up on career progression, or even on their career altogether – especially if they have the 'pull' of children they could be caring for instead.

It doesn't help that there is not really a 'sisterhood' – the women who make it are not always supporting other women behind them (and, worse, sometimes even undermining them), while men are supporting and promoting their male 'mini-mes'.

Nor does it help that women who try to apply strategies to win at work that work for men are often criticised and disliked, by men and women. And not being liked is not something most women enjoy or aspire to.

All of these things create the Invisible Ceiling for women – you can't see it, but it is there.

There are not many women like the Super 7% who make it to CEO or equivalent, who do some of the smart things men do and much more. They are an incredible combination of not just intelligence and competence, but 'Authentic Women' who have been strong enough to stay themselves, self-aware enough to know and leverage their personal strengths (including working with and managing people) and to know the kind of environment and culture in which they will thrive and succeed. They have huge strength and resilience and are not paralysed by fear of failure, with a healthy 'it's only work' attitude, clear strategies for handling men and thus no fear of (or need to fear) them and no heavy household or childcare burden to carry. These amazing women who have this rich combination are a very rare species – and if we are waiting for women to be all of these things in order to get their fair share of big roles then the bar is too high versus the men's and it is no wonder men keep winning this race.

There are also some things that I believe men do better than most women at work, some 'laws of the professional jungle' that men know and do and (most) women don't. I have been in many senior level meetings with men and women and, as I became more and more aware of the gender diversity issue, I started to really observe how men handled discussions and conflict in comparison to women. Of course I witnessed the results of the invisible force of the male-dominated culture, but I saw more than this. I saw the way the men made difficult points that could have been inflammatory in a very smooth and diplomatic way that engaged the room, whereas the women would often (once they mustered the courage and energy to go for it and make a controversial point) do so in a rather sharp and damaging way that ruffled feathers and led to an unconstructive discussion (not following Lois P Frankel's advice in *Nice Girls Don't Get the Corner Office* to 'Disagree without being disagreeable').[3] I'm not saying that all the men I ever saw in meetings stayed totally calm at all times, but when they didn't it seemed they were much more comfortable expressing their anger. It made them seem like strong leaders in contrast to the women who felt red-faced shame and embarrassment at becoming angry (girls and women have fewer female role models for expressing healthy anger). The men generally handled these things better than women, avoiding open conflict and managing difficult things one-to-one.

I have also seen the way that the men could have a passionate disagreement in a meeting, but it didn't stop them from 'staying mates'. I was fascinated to read Sir Oliver Letwin describe Boris Johnson as 'a perfectly charming man' throughout their extremely tense discussions and disagreements.[4] I don't think there is any question that the smooth, matey 'male' way of handling these things is superior. I believe it stems from the fact that men don't take it as personally as some women do, and they are able to separate work from the personal and leave emotion out of it. They see business and work as just a game and they play it as such. So many men over the years have told me this, that what we do at work is not in itself that important and so they are fundamentally just playing and having fun, that I shouldn't take it so seriously or so personally. Many women don't see it this way and take it very seriously and, as a result of their passion and attachment to the cause, ironically potentially manage things less well. And, if work is just a game, we can argue that men are likely to be much better at it than women because we know they have had a lot more practice from playing sport and games from when they were boys. Perhaps boys didn't just learn leadership and resilience and confidence, but also years of practice and experience in being in groups and influencing others on controversial things without damaging the friendship. Perhaps women, who for sure didn't play as much sport as girls or play as much in general, have not developed their skills as much as boys/men in working in groups and managing difficult moments and controversial discussions in a constructive way. This dynamic may also of course not just have affected women, but also some men who didn't develop the same skills as other boys from not playing as much sport. Is this possibly why we see women staying quiet in meetings but boiling with frustration and eventually exploding with emotion and passion (I was personally called 'too passionate' by a company President once) because they can't hold it in anymore? Which is arguably not as controlled and thus not as impressive as it could be. Have we simply not learnt and practised the skills needed in these situations as much as boys have? When Laura Bates tells us in *Everyday Sexism* that 'When male MPs disagree, it's described as just that – a disagreement', whereas female MPs are described as 'bickering women' in a 'catfight',[5] should we dismiss this as simply a sexist statement, or should we look a little deeper and accept that maybe, just maybe, just sometimes, men handle things better than women do?

One thing men also seem to handle better is the hierarchy and their place in it. One man told me that he feels very uncomfortable with women in authority who overtly leverage their senior position to influence an outcome and that he couldn't think of a male leader who managed things this way. Some women may feel more need to 'flex their authority muscles' than men do, for all the reasons we have discussed – but if the result is a male leadership style that is less jarring, more comfortable and better respected by those on the end of it then, again, we should take note and learn from this.

Men are also better at self-marketing and networking – they are savvier than women when it comes to understanding that stellar performance is just table stakes and the importance of relationship currency. They carve out time in the day to invest in this, while the women are focusing on being as 'efficient' as possible with their time. Frustrating for the ones who are churning through more work, but men are winning and getting the big roles and promotions, so who is ultimately being the smartest here? Yes, men have more time to network for all the reasons we have discussed but, let's be honest, even if men were carrying an equal share of the work at home and women had more time, most would still dislike and avoid doing it and men would still win on this.

Men also understand that work requires not just performance but also... 'performance'. They know it isn't school and about getting top grades, that they don't know everything (nobody does) and they are comfortable with that, and it doesn't stop them from feeling confident and therefore from performing confidently. They are not afraid of failure and have no aspiration to be perfect, because they know that it doesn't exist – they accept that sometimes they will need to 'wing it' and fill in the inevitable gaps, and that is not a problem (it's all part of the fun).

Women have a lot less experience in the professional jungle of work over the decades and in the manoeuvring and politics that are inevitable, particularly in a large organisation. Their naivety in just focusing on the job and not playing the game hurts them and holds them back from making as much progress as they could or should.

Men also have had a lot more role models to learn from on all of this than women. One of my great friends shared with me a really interesting example of the importance of this role-modelling plays in teaching us (or not) how to handle things. She is very much an example of a very strong woman who had never faced gender issues in the early years of her career – but when she was made CEO of her company, the gender diversity issue hit her head on. In a meeting she was not aligned with another senior man in the same company and his approach was to try to bully her into agreeing. She felt uncomfortable with his aggression but fought back and assertively closed him down. I don't believe any of this would have happened between two men or two women – with another man he would have known to manage it in a 'buddy' way and would have avoided a public confrontation. She similarly would not have managed it this way with another woman. I asked her what she would have done if he had been, for example, me and she didn't have to think for more than one second about the answer – we would never have got into that public confrontation because as soon as we realised we had a potential disagreement we would have picked up the phone or grabbed a coffee and sorted it out between us. Men have a lot of role models for and experience of managing issues with men, and women have this with women, but there are not yet enough role model 'set plays' for this kind of scenario between men and women for us to learn from and replicate.

Men don't win at work because they are inherently better, more intelligent or more capable. But they have been playing and practising this game called work a lot, lot longer than women have and as things stand, they are still getting significantly more practice and experience and will continue to unless some important and profound things change to break the self-fulfilling prophecy of male dominance at senior levels in all arenas. Women need to have their fair share of the senior jobs and of the seats at the table, for the benefit of us all.

14

And now what the hell are we going to do about it?

IT'S INCREDIBLE REALLY, isn't it, when you really think about it? We have all these brilliant women not being leveraged by their companies and organisations, despite the best women being good as the best men – and despite all the improvements that diversity would make to their performance, their businesses, their organisations, their countries, their lives. How can we keep letting this happen? How can women go on accepting this as 'just the way it is' and watch as our lives and world are run by men?

There are some big reasons why we let it happen. Firstly, not everyone has truly internalised that gender diversity is a win for all, and that progress is in everyone's best interests. Thucydides taught us that people change for three reasons – honour, fear or self-interest. Until we as a society truly and deeply feel a reason to change then nothing will because, as Iris Bohnet says in *Gender Equality by Design*:

> Put bluntly, changing behaviour means work that the vast majority of us are not motivated to do.[1]

And, my goodness, we need to be motivated to do this work because it's intensely tough, driven as it is by so many unconscious, invisible and cultural forces. But we absolutely must address these forces. Things are not going to change on their own by letting things play out and run their course. 'The master's tools will never dismantle the master's house' in Audre Lorde's words.[2] The patriarchy will, even if unconsciously, continue to reassert itself and protect the status quo. Without serious intervention, the invisible, unconscious forces will keep pulling the strings and feeding the self-fulfilling prophecy and someone in 100 years will be writing *Why Men Still Win at Work*. What a waste of 100 years that would be for us all.

So, the question is, how to make the unconscious conscious and how to prevent it from influencing our decisions? How do we ensure we reward and promote people based on objectivity, not bias? How do we intervene collectively and sustainably to remove the Invisible Ceiling for women to help them to start winning at work, and reap the rewards for us all of doing this?

The good news is that it is possible. The UN is one organisation that is showing us the way. UN General Assembly President María Fernanda Espinosa praised the leap towards full gender parity at the UN under Secretary-General António Guterres, saying it was

> testament to the fact that when there is a political will, and leadership, it is possible... For the first time in history, the UN Senior Management Group is comprised of more women than men.[3]

And developing countries are taking steps (more than developed countries in fact) to promote gender equality in parliament and similar governing bodies. In India, there has been a requirement since the 1990s that women are represented on at least a third of village councils.[4] Rwanda is the first country to have a female majority in parliament (44 of the 80 seats are held by women).[5] At Burberry and Rightmove 50% of the board are women. And many other organisations are committed to equality – at the end of 2018, 45 international music festivals and conferences signed a pledge towards achieving or maintaining a 50/50 gender balance in performers across their festivals by 2022.

So how do we intervene to drive gender equality? First of all, the answer is *not* just being aware of the issue. Being aware doesn't lead us to change our behaviours. Sadly, even really understanding and caring about this issue and wanting to fix it doesn't in itself make a difference. (Iris Bohnet reminds us of how much we all care about not wasting electricity but leave hotel lights on when we exit the room anyway – and the thing that made a difference was not beginning to care but the manual invention of key card light activation.)[6] The answer is also *not* putting your whole organisation through diversity training – it simply doesn't work. US companies spend $300 million a year on diversity training but an analysis of 800 US companies from 1971 to 2002 showed that diversity training had no relationship to the diversity of the workforce. Another review of 830 US companies even found that diversity training exercises were followed by a 7.5% drop in the number of women in management.[7] Professor Frank Dobbin and Alexandra Kalev, sociologists at Harvard and Tel Aviv Universities, studied 800 companies and concluded that 'your organisation will become less diverse, not more, if you require managers to go to diversity training.'[8] Over 20 studies have proven that trying to suppress gender inequality doesn't work; in Helena Morrissey's words, 'we cannot instruct people to alter their thought processes and their attitudes.'[9]

The answer cannot be that women need to work even harder and put in excessive hours and face time they do not have in order to be noticed and well-perceived. People need rest and recuperation and there are already too many burnout victims in this world, so please let's not look to add more. Nor can we accept that the answer be that a woman has to either not have kids, so she has time for the work or find a 'supportive, non-emasculated husband'. There's nothing wrong with choosing these options (and good for those women who find these amazing and rare men) but, let's face it, this isn't a realistic solution for most women. There must be a way for women to have families and get the support they need so they can succeed – without relying on finding a certain type of man or funding an expensive nanny.

The answer to driving gender equality is not just for women to be stronger and take responsibility, rise up and 'lean in'. As Michelle Obama has said, 'It's not always enough… because that doesn't work all the time.'[10] Zaid Al-Qassab of Channel 4 more provocatively said:

> I don't like the Lean In concept, it's not the solution, it's just a sticking plaster.

Of course, women must step up when they can and avoid having a victim mentality, but it's unhelpful when people suggest that it is women who hold the key to fixing it. Women talking to women about gender inequality isn't going to get us very far and if only women take on this revolution then it will never take hold. We need men to understand this issue and realise it's important for them too to take action and drive interventions. Men dominate and own the culture and the decisions, and therefore only they can really change it. They have the positions and the power. Women cannot take it from them, they have to decide to share it.

The answer is not for us to ask women to stop being women and act like men. It isn't going to happen, and it shouldn't. Unlike Lois P Frankel in *Nice Girls Don't Get the Corner Office*, I do not believe the answer is for women not to apply lipstick or touch their hair in meetings or show any signs of emotion in front of men.[11] As Kezia Dugdale, ex-Member of the Scottish Parliament for Lothian says, 'What's the point in electing women to Parliament if they have to act like men to survive?'[12] We could ask the same question in all jobs – the whole point is that diversity is good because it brings… diversity! Diversity means difference – different opinions, different angles – which we will only get if we create an environment in which people can be themselves.

The reality is that none of these things will work because

of the huge invisible issues I have discussed. We must not underestimate how deep and powerful our unconscious bias is, and it will therefore require equally powerful conscious work to counter it. Just awareness, just caring, just training is never going to be enough.[13] We are going to need to ask people to change their unconscious thoughts and attitudes. This is going to be a hell of a lot of hard work.

Are you ready and motivated to do this work? Here's my To Do lists for you if you want to make gender equality a reality in your world – wherever you are, whatever your gender, wherever you work.

To Do lists

Parents and teachers

Hillevi Engström, ex-Member of Swedish Parliament, said we need to 'start in kindergarten' and she's right.[1] The earlier we start influencing the unconscious the better.

Never give your daughters and young girls any reason to question that they can do and achieve anything that boys can do. Teach your sons and young boys from the start that girls are equal and should be listened to and respected in exactly the same way as boys and men. If you hear any sexist comments from your boys (even if masquerading as a joke), don't tolerate it.

Listen carefully to your daughters and young girls. Listen for their different view on things – especially if they have brothers and are already in a male-dominated environment. Don't make her feel bad or wrong for experiencing things or expressing their emotions differently. Let them be themselves.

Don't make girls feel that the most important thing in life is to always deliver perfect work and get top grades, and encourage them not to be afraid of making mistakes or being told off. Treat boys and girls the same, and emphasise that their academic successes aren't the be all and end all, and that their imperfections are natural, something to learn from rather than a source of shame and embarrassment.

Make sure that playing and having fun is a big part of their lives, not just schoolwork.

 Get your daughters and young girls playing sport. Do everything you can to keep them playing it when they (inevitably) lose interest when they hit their teenage years. A little shameless pitch for netball here (I confess I'm biased) – it's a fantastic sport for girls because it is a highly skilful and competitive team game that they can enjoy and stick with (often throughout their lives) and that they can play without the interference and domination of boys. It is also non-contact so not too off-puttingly aggressive.

And an extra one for dads

When you debate with your daughters, teach them to keep arguing and pushing to the end. Don't teach them to fear your anger and to back off because you may get or are getting angry – if you do, you may be teaching them to do this with all men for the rest of their lives.

Media makers and providers

Role models are so important. As Stella Creasy MP says, 'Too often women aren't being considered as capable leaders because our concept of what leadership is defined by our history rather than our future.'[2] What we have experienced and seen people doing informs our unconscious beliefs about what people can do. It's a self-fulfilling prophecy and we need to see counter-stereotypical role models to break it. You as media makers and providers have a critical role, maybe the most important role of all, in deciding the female role models that society sees.

Show positive female role models in your TV programmes and films. Give them 50% of the screen time and dialogue. Show them as lawyers and judges, politicians and Prime Ministers, CEOs, mathematicians, scientists, engineers, astronauts, whatever. It will start to undo decades of women being seen as stereotypical mother, wife or sex object and embedded in the male subconscious as such. This sends a message to every young girl out there that someone like her can do these jobs. As the Geena Davis Institute on Gender in Media goes, 'If she can see it, she can be it.'[3]

Represent women and women's journalism in your newspapers and newsfeeds. Let people read and hear the female view on the world as much as the male one. Sign up to the BBC's 50:50 Project, which aims to create journalism and media content that fairly and equally represents our world by improving the visibility of women. This methodology, which leverages data on gender representation, has been adopted by over 60 other organisations around the world.

Show women's sport on TV. The 2019 Women's World Cup coverage (certainly what I saw in France and the UK) was brilliant. It's fantastic to see netball starting to get more airtime too – one of my highlights of the year in 2018 was seeing the England netball team winning Team of the Year at the BBC Sports Personality of the Year awards – and sports moment of the year! It is important for everyone to see women in this way – not in the usual, stereotypical, perfectly groomed and sexy role but focusing 100% on playing their sport and competing with their team. It's important for girls and women to play sport and for men and boys to see this side of them too.

Organisations and businesses

If you are committed to tackling this then buckle up, you've got a lot of work ahead. You're going to need to forget about trying to change minds – you won't. Manual intervention is what is needed: you're going to need to 'design in' structural and process interventions that will help you to make non-gender-biased decisions without having to think about it. 'Designs that make it easier for our biased minds to get it right' in Iris Bohnet's words.[4] It will be hard work but it will be worth it: in the future, the organisations that don't change will not be able to compete for and keep the best female talent and they will lose out to the ones, like you, who do – and, as a consequence, you will be rewarded with significantly and sustainably better results.

Recruiters

Write your ads carefully to appeal to women. Bear in mind the leading business school brochure that used words like 'dominate' and 'world-beating' and found only one woman applied. Remember that men know that they can apply for jobs without meeting all the criteria in your ad, but many women don't – so use language like 'If you meet even some of these criteria, we would welcome your application'. Make manual interventions in your recruitment process to ensure you look beyond gender and counter the inevitable unconscious bias towards men. If you feel you have a big unconscious bias issue, request gender-neutral CVs and applications. And remember to ask yourself the question 'Who will best complete the team?' to avoid hiring the same type of person over and over again.

Ban the F word: 'fit'. If someone 'fits' it means they look and behave like the majority in a dominant culture. Looking for 'fit' will get you the opposite of diversity.

Set a gender equality goal and make a plan that changes systems and processes to deliver it. You get what you measure or, put another way, what does not get measured does not get fixed. Measure the results, reward people who deliver, fire people who consistently don't. Just like you would with a business goal.

There are two social issues where companies have genuinely improved in the last 30 years: workplace accidents and corruption. This is because they started measuring their performance and gave bonuses to managers who improved and fired managers who didn't.

Measure people too. Really look at and focus on their results and performance metrics, not your or others' intuition about or perceptions of them (which will inevitably be based on unconscious and invisible gender forces). Too many companies pay lip service to this – they go through the motions of reviewing results but don't follow through and give the best ratings and jobs to the people with the best results. This too often allows their human instinct and personal evaluation to have the final say and often, unfortunately, rewards the ones that are not actually the best people.

 Hire and measure leaders on the extent to which they display inclusive leadership behaviours. Reward those who are leading inclusively. Russell Reynolds Associates Diversity & Inclusion research shows that leaders who manage diversity well have heightened emotional intelligence and behave differently in comparison to average ones:[5]

- They gather input on D&I pain points from the organisation
- They proactively create time and space for open and welcoming discussions around D&I
- They seek input from diverse backgrounds and perspectives
- They proactively challenge bias, intolerance and resistance to change
- They create D&I focused roles and policies and use a scorecard to track progress
- They take time to understand the working experience for each direct report and peer
- They recognise and celebrate the diverse identities of their workforce
- They continuously seek insights from different individuals and challenge their own and others' existing mindsets, they are curious to learn about and use new approaches.

Hire and promote people into manager roles who understand the value of treating people as people and naturally want to help others succeed. Measure them on how well they retain, engage and develop people (this means you are going to need to ask and listen to the people!). Value and reward your great managers – for managing this well, not just their business results.

Ensure you have an active 'trawling' process, so you are always looking 'beneath the umbrella', not just at the superficial, or relying on your personal perception. Talented leaders are sometimes not visible to their seniors (if they are not good at self-marketing and networking) but are more visible to their peers and subordinates.

Are you proactively trawling and asking the junior people what they think of their leaders to look for your point of view to be changed? Think how often you have seen someone promoted when the people who work for them think they are a waste of space.

In *The Business*, Iain Banks creates a system of voting for your management:

> We have had several expensive but unpublished studies performed by highly respected universities and business colleges, which have tended to support our belief that letting people vote for their bosses means that a greater proportion of able and gifted people flourish and rise using this method than any other. The more usual systems, where people are picked out from above... leads to more problems than it solves, producing a culture where those on any given level within a company are constantly trying to find ways to flatter those above them, sabotage the careers of their colleagues... and generally spend far too much time frivolously furthering their own selfish ends and their status within the company when they ought rightfully to be engaged in the more serious and productive pursuit of making all concerned more money. Gaining promotion by fooling your boss... can be relatively easy. Gaining the trust of those who work with you every day

and will have to take orders from you if you are promoted is a lot more difficult.[6]

This from a work of fiction, but I couldn't have put it better myself and it's not a bad idea for the real world! A trawling or voting process would systematically seek out feedback from the junior people in the organisation on who they saw as the strongest and most talented leaders and integrate this into decisions on role allocations and promotions. This does still need to be managed with awareness. My previous company had a 360° feedback process, but nobody ever gave anything but positive or neutral feedback for fear of repercussions, so if a manager had already made up their mind on their 'star' employee they were not going to find anything in the feedback to jolt their perception. Notwithstanding this, a well-managed and well-devised 360° appraisal or trawling system that is non-threatening and respects anonymity and confidentiality is a powerful intervention mechanism to override unconscious bias.

Remember that this is not just about promotions and ensuring women get their fair share of them, that's just the tip of the iceberg. You also need to ensure that women are not just represented numerically at the same level as men but are given the same job and project scope, team size and quality, and budgets in order to make their work and contribution fully comparable. Have you unconsciously put your men on the big businesses and the women on the smaller ones that you are less worried about? Or even into 'side' functions instead of on the core business? This frequently happens. Wharton School's Janice

Fanning Madden found that female stockbrokers were on inferior and worse accounts with lower sales opportunities and, as a result, earning 60% of the male accounts.[7] I remember one of the women I most admired at my previous company finally demanding a 'crucible' role on a big business that would allow her to show what she could do and that she was ready for the next level. Good for her – but in my experience not many women do this, and most men don't have to because, if they are competent and confident, the big jobs come naturally. So, remember that women are as competent and capable as the men (even if they don't seem as confident) and give women the toughest assignments, not the easiest ones. Put them front of stage in the important roles and let them show what they can do.

Make sure there are at least two female candidates for each role or promotion. Ideally there should be as many female candidates as male. I've seen people patting themselves on the back when they have one female candidate, but this is simply not enough, and the woman easily becomes the 'token' to be eliminated.

Get a reliable system in place for managing sexual harassment issues well. Women are wary of taking on a sexual harassment issue directly as HR are unlikely to take action against a senior, valued (and expensive to dispose of) man and it will ultimately be them who is damaged. This is simply a disgrace – find a system to fix it that people feel secure to use.

Intervene and tackle the salary gap. Sir Philip Hampton said of the gender pay gap that women 'let it happen'.[8] I think it would be more accurate to say that women are behaving as women do and men are behaving as men do, and that this leads to more of the money in men's hands, regardless of ability and contribution. It has been shown that when women are given the opportunity to negotiate their salary in a more transparent environment, they will take it, so there is a big push for the solution to be that salaries are made fully transparent so discrepancies cannot be hidden.

On one hand, this does force a fix but, for me, it doesn't address the core issue, which is why does this happen, why do we pay men a higher salary? In my view, in larger organisations, your Chief Diversity Officer (oh yes, by the way, you need one of these if you don't have one already!) needs to go beyond making salary transparent and should have 'salary equality' as a key responsibility, closely and regularly monitoring women's salaries in comparison to that of their male peers. When they see a gap that cannot be justified by a difference in level, tenure or scope, the flashing amber light should go on to flag that this is highly likely to be a case of gender bias (probably unconscious) from the woman's manager. There then needs to be follow-up with that manager, investigation into why this has happened and intervention – starting with equalisation of the salary, and fast.

Don't underestimate the importance of you being intentional about this. It is extremely demotivating for a woman to discover she is paid less than a man for doing an equivalent job. It is one of the things that make a woman feel she is not valued and, ultimately, that she should leave you – or even her career.

Be brave and make radical interventions to free up time for your employees to do the other things they need to do outside work without causing them sleep deprivation, stress and illness. For example, disable company communications from 6pm to 9am and at weekends, force people to take their holidays and leave their laptops and iPads locked in their desk when they do. This may sound radical, but it would be a great equaliser for those with household and childcare duties to take care of and, if your CEO and company really, really buys in to the evidence that gender diversity drives results, then you absolutely would have the courage to do this because you know you will benefit hugely from it.

 Give fully paid paternity leave and encourage (even enforce) it being taken. Paternity leave is a critical gender equality enabler – if dads have more time to bond with a new child and are more involved in caring for their children right from the start, this can set a pattern that lasts long after the leave ends. In one study of working fathers in the US, those who took leave of two weeks or more were significantly more likely to be actively involved in their child's care (feeding, getting up in the night, changing nappies) nine months after birth.[9] Fathers who take more leave also share family chores more equally. When men increase their use of paternity leave, studies show that the amount of household work fathers and mothers do becomes more gender balanced over time, with the men contributing more hours per day. Also, when fathers take more paternity leave, it increases the ability of mothers to engage in paid work.[10] One study in Canada found mothers increase their level of full-time work and a study in Sweden found similar positive impacts on women's labour force participation.[11]

It is also critical that the paternity leave is long enough – survey data shows that nine out of ten US fathers take some time off work for the birth or adoption of a child, but 70% of fathers take ten days of leave or less.[12] This is simply not enough to change cultural norms about gender, work and household responsibilities. It's also critical that the leave is paid – in surveys, men say they are much more likely to take leave if it is paid, no doubt because they need the money (especially if they are in the 'breadwinner' role) but also because this legitimises it in their mind (many men have been embarrassed to take unpaid leave while other men keep on working). I also believe that significant paid paternity leave, if it were to become the norm, could eliminate some of the gender bias against pregnant women (or even just women of an age at which they may get pregnant at some point) that we still see in some workplaces, where women are not chosen for the big role or promotion because they might need to go on maternity leave soon. This becomes neutralised in a world where a man is as likely to need paternity leave as a woman is to need maternity leave.

Some are leading the way, including Diageo who announced in 2019 that all UK employees are eligible for 52 weeks parental leave (26 paid), regardless of gender and in Sweden they typically offer 6 to 17 weeks of paid paternity leave.[13] P&G Switzerland, to their credit, have recently introduced 8 weeks of paid paternity leave, as do some major tech firms, going beyond what the Swiss law requires. They previously had a lesser paternity leave policy in place, but a limited number of men have made use of it; now they want to create a culture where it is normal for a new father to consider and take paternity leave. They are convinced that this will increase the probability that parenting will be equal in the family.

What I can tell you is that I have two male friends who have recently taken paternity leave and have both described the experience as life-changing and one that has given them a whole new level of understanding of and respect for their wives and the mothers of their (very tiring) babies.

 Ensure you have parental policies that are truly applicable for men as well as women – and that men are encouraged equally to leverage them. Don't let flexible working hours or working from home be seen as only 'mum policies' and for those who are less committed to their career – this undermines women in general and the men who are willing to take on their share of the parental work.

Be aware of what is important to women at work and do everything you can to meet their expectations and needs, which are not always the same as men's and not just about 'the work'. GALLUP® asked US workers who were considering a job change or who had recently switched employers to indicate how important particular factors are and women placed the highest importance on 'the ability to do what they do best' – two-thirds of female employees believe this is 'very important' versus 55% of male employees; 60% of women rate work-life balance and personal wellbeing as 'very important', compared with 48% of men; 39% of women say the reputation of the company is 'very important' to them, versus 33% of men; and 32% of women say the company's cause is 'very important' versus only 22% of men. The last one is another invisible force but a very important one for women. As the GALLUP® report says:

> Women want their work to matter and have meaning… Women want to feel connected to their company… They care about values, and they care about purpose and cause… Women want to know that their company has an impact on society and they play a part.[14]

We have talked a lot about men's 'it's not personal, it's just work' attitude and that women can to an extent learn from this, but companies and organisations also need to accept that many women will and do take work more personally, simply because of the way they are made. 'Women want to develop meaningful relationships. They want to work with people they like, admire, trust, respect and have fun with. They make friends with colleagues, customers and clients. Women need to feel like someone appreciates and likes them.[15] If you can create a work culture and environment that meets women's need for work-life balance, personal wellbeing, meaning, connection and relationships then you will have a good chance of keeping their loyalty and staying ahead of your competition in the battle for their talent. Be aware that childcare and flexible working are not the only issues. If you tackle and address them it is not 'job done', not by a long way.

Create a gender balanced environment where everyone, whatever their gender or approach, feels comfortable, relaxed and confident to be their authentic self. Ensure no one feels a need to copy the dominant people and styles in an attempt to fit in. It's not just about the numbers and it's not enough just to have women on your team – you need to have an environment and culture that enables them to perform at their best; you need 'engaged diversity', not just diversity. Remember that 'when people understand and apply their strengths, the effect on their lives and work is transformational. Individuals who use their strengths every day are three times more likely to say they have an excellent quality of life' and have 'higher levels of employee engagement and performance, and they are less likely than other employees to leave their organisations.'[16] 'The bottom line is that women need to know that their company values them for what they bring'. Make use of a tool like CliftonStrengths® to enable your people to understand their strengths and create a culture that encourages and enables them to use them.

Set up a strong and sustainable sponsorship system. Not mentoring, sponsorship. Mentors are all well and good, but they usually play a coaching and advisory role which may be more useful for those who are already strong in networking, career-building and knowing when and where to seek a bit of help and advice (and who have or make the time for this in the busy working day). A true sponsor, however, will go beyond this and proactively support their 'sponsee', prompting them to go for opportunities, suggesting them for roles and advocating for them for positions and promotions – they will actually put themselves on the line for someone. We could all use a sponsor or two in our lives, but I would argue that women need them the most, given all of the confidence and risk-taking demons they are dealing with.

Accept and embrace the 50/50 approach. It is controversial but it is the thing that I believe you must do if you truly believe in and want to achieve gender equality in your organisation. Even if you do all of the other things, it isn't going to be enough. I used to be one of the people who wholeheartedly rejected this concept and there are many, many others who do. But after what I have seen and what I have learnt over the last few years, I have become convinced. The invisible, unconscious dynamics are too strong, too deep and too powerful for women to overcome without equally powerful intervention to help. We are stuck in a self-fulfilling prophecy and we need to break out of it. Just like in a business situation, where big issues need big and bold interventions rather than polite, gentle, patient ones, this issue needs the same.

Now, I am very aware of all the arguments against 50/50, not least 'the anxiety about positive discrimination' as Helena Morrissey calls it. How many times have I heard from men that 'Quotas don't work, we should hire the best candidates'?[17] or 'As long as the woman got the job on merit'. I must say this assumption that appointing women means lowering standards makes me furious – how dare they think this, let alone say it out loud? I know, of course, that they say it because they believe it, they believe that men are better (for all the reasons we have been through) and – ironically this very response is perhaps the biggest giveaway that we need to take the 50/50 approach – because without an intervention like this, no matter what else we do, when it comes to the moment where the decision is made (usually by a man, let's face it) about who gets the job or promotion then the decision will be biased towards the male candidate. We simply won't get to 50/50 naturally, and we need to get there, not only to reap the benefits of gender equality and diversity but so that we all get used to seeing women in these leadership roles – so the women who succeed pave the way for others to follow. We also know that women need critical mass to be heard and to succeed; as Laura Liswood says in *The Loudest Duck*, when women get to 50% or close 'the dominant group is forced to take the other's perspective seriously… The mice have to be numerous enough for the elephants to notice and change.'[18] So what do I mean by the 50/50 approach? I mean commit to a 50/50 gender split. Don't settle for less, don't be satisfied with being in 'The 30% Club', why would you be?

 Commit to 50/50 at all levels, including at the executive and board level. You only change the culture of a place when you change the top. Be intentional about delivering it, not in five years but with urgency from today. Put in place all of the interventions above to enable it, measure yourselves and your leaders against delivering it, reward those who do and penalise those who don't, and accept no excuses for anyone not delivering. We have seen that brilliant, competent, talented women are out there in the same force as the men. Anyone who isn't finding them simply isn't trying.

When you get women into the leadership roles, go all out and celebrate them visibly as role models. It is so important that we all don't only see men in these roles. 'If people are biased against female leaders and never see a woman in a leadership position, they can never update their beliefs'.[19] Women role models make a big difference. A study of 20,000 US companies from 1990 to 2003 showed that when the share of top female managers increased, the share of women in mid-level management increased.[20] Kathleen McGinn and Katherine Milkman of Harvard & Wharton Business School showed that female attorneys are more likely to rise through the ranks when they have female partners and role models.[21] A US law firm also found that retention of their junior female employees was highly correlated with the number of female supervisors.

Remember that all the women in your company or organisation are watching how women are treated and taking note. They may not say anything, but they are registering it and understanding that this is the way they will be treated one day, so make sure what they see from you is something they want to stay around for.

Managers

In addition to implementing all of the interventions your organisation commits to, you have a few extra things on your To Do list.

 Access to you is precious – be fair with it. Be aware that men will generally be much more aware of the importance of making themselves and their work visible to you and will therefore be much more proactive about booking and finding time with you, while the women are more 'heads down' and focusing on delivering their work. If you just spend time with whoever books a meeting or coffee in your calendar and let things happen without intervention, I hope you realise by now how that will play out – you will see more of the men and you will as a result feel more comfortable with them and unconsciously come to believe that they are stronger or better. So don't be passive about your time, intervene, be proactive as a manager about ensuring you spend as much time on talking with and reviewing the work of your female employees as you do for the men. Ask yourself at the beginning of every week who is booked into your diary this week and, if needed, intervene. Ask yourself at the end of each week who you have spent time with and, if you haven't talked with your women managers, intervene and book in a catch-up. Always remember that the people you know best are not always the best people.

Keep aware that women do not hear things in the same way that men do (remember 'negative allusion' versus 'positive allusion'?). It simply doesn't work to talk to women and men in the same way, or to give feedback in the same way – you are giving the men another invisible advantage. Try the technique of asking, 'What did you hear me say?' after giving input or feedback to a woman. You will probably be surprised, then you can adjust the message to the (no doubt more positive) one that you actually wanted to give – and learn for next time how to do it differently.

Allow for the fact that women are generally not as comfortable as men discussing their salary. So pay extra attention to ensuring they are being paid the same as to their male peers and the men's salary has not been unconsciously driven ahead as a result of more pushing and focus from them. Are you certain that the women who work for you have the same salary as their male equivalents? When was the last time you checked? Next time a man asks you for a pay rise and you give it, check your women's salary is keeping up. And when a woman does attempt to broach the issue, make sure you don't react negatively because this is not 'expected' behaviour. In these kinds of situations, always ask yourself how you would feel and react if it was a man in front of you doing and saying exactly the same thing. The same goes for career expectations – women will generally not be as comfortable as men with putting these out there. So, don't wait for them to do this and assume they're not ambitious or interested in progression if they do not; you need to instigate regular career discussions with your female employees and ask them what role they would like to do next or in the future. If you don't you may never find out what they are thinking before it is too late. Remember that women will not necessarily tell you that they are frustrated about being under-utilised, or being given more responsibility without the promotion, or being passed over for promotion, or not getting the salary they deserve. They may seem to tolerate it but under the surface the frustration is mounting and any day you may be caught totally by surprise by their resignation letter.

It may be unrealistic to create a true meritocracy due to basic human nature and all of the invisible and unconscious gender forces at play. But at least ensure that you do not, as a manager, create an 'illusion of meritocracy'. Make sure all employees are coached on how things work, what influences perceptions of people beyond performance, what influences decisions about who gets jobs and promotions – otherwise the men will understand this, many of the women will not and will be at a big disadvantage.

 Don't be conned by the people who play it (and you) well but are not delivering on the work when you are not watching. The people in your team will be very aware of this but probably won't feel they can tell you because you have been charmed by these people and, quite simply, you like them. An old friend and I used to classify everyone in our previous company as either 'surfers or haymakers'; make it your job to know the difference, who is in which group and to ensure you reward the haymakers and set the surfers out to sea!

Be on full alert in meetings for the gender dynamics. Resist being impressed by the men who dominate the airtime, who don't listen to and interrupt the women and maybe even repeat their points with a big dose of gravitas and self-confidence. Watch and listen to the women (you will probably need to listen more carefully to hear them and their point). Encourage them to speak and, when they do, don't tolerate them being cut off – tell everyone that you are interested in their point and want to hear them finish it. And be aware of a silent woman who is not speaking or participating – I can promise you, it is not because she doesn't have ideas or something to say.

Before the To Do lists for women and men, a word to both on dress code

This is a tricky one. The way we dress is one of our greatest ways of expressing our individual, authentic selves. Personally, not much bores me more than seeing people dress in the same old, expected way and I can't help my own unconscious bias that 'boring clothes equal boring mind'. Telling someone how to dress is tantamount to withdrawing their freedom, so I am not going to tell women what they should or should not wear. However, we cannot ignore that every one of my Super 7% interviewees believes that there is a 'work uniform' for women – and for men – which sends out unconscious messages of professionalism. I think women and men have some things to think about here.

Women: we need to accept some biological facts that will not change – (heterosexual) men look at women's bodies, if they get the chance, even if they don't want to. This is not your fault or responsibility, but it is your problem – because if you are displaying your physical assets, the reality is this may be a distraction from the highly intelligent and important thing you are saying being heard and remembered. This is your choice, but don't be naïve about the impact and if you make this choice, make it a conscious one.

Men: this is your problem and your responsibility – whatever a woman is wearing, you need to learn to deal with the fact it is absolutely possible for her to be sexually attractive AND also very good at her job. She is not 'mother' or 'wife' or 'mistress' or 'whatever' or 'manager' or 'leader' – she is multifaceted and can be all of these things at the same time. And all that matters are the things she is saying and the work she is doing – so please, be professional and put the rest to one side in the workplace.

Women

Having said that I get irritated when people push the gender equality problem onto women's shoulders, there are some things that I do believe women need to open their eyes to and get comfortable with – because men are our competition for the jobs and the promotions that we want and, just like any competition, we need to observe them, learn from them and work out the things they do that we need to match them on (POPs – Points of Parity) as well as where we can leverage our strengths and be better (PODs – Points of Difference). Men can't fix this for us alone, we have some work to do. So, to all the women out there:

Be aware of your level of self-confidence. Be aware that your lack of it is an unfounded self-perception with no correlation to your competence, intelligence or ability versus others. As Eleanor Roosevelt said, 'No one can make you feel inferior without your consent.'[22] Including yourself.

Accept the reality that at senior levels, everyone is winging it sometimes and putting on a performance – the men too. It is natural for everyone to feel nerves in a big meeting and to be a bit scared to make a point. But if it is an important point, you must make it. You have a duty to your company or organisation to make it – this is what you are paid for. So, you need to 'woman up', take a deep breath and perform with confidence.

Reframe your imposter syndrome as humility and thoroughness. It is something that is positive and useful to you, a competitive advantage that makes you check and probe things more deeply and thoroughly, that helps you learn and grow. It is something that can give you confidence in your output and contribution.

Say goodbye to perfectionism and make friends with failure. Remember Winston Churchill's words, 'Success is not final, failure is not fatal: it is the courage to continue that counts.' If you didn't learn it at school or from sport, then learn it now. Failure is a natural part of life and work; it is something to learn from and you must not let it be a paralyser and stop you from trying or achieving things. The people who win at work know that they are not perfect, that nobody is, that they will fail sometimes because everybody does – and this is what liberates them to move forwards and upwards.

Ask yourself, are you your partner's servant? Are you one of the many women who is taking on an unequal share of household tasks and childcare, causing you not to have enough time for your job, or for your rest and sleep. Please address this before it's too late. If you are both in paid work, you should be sharing the unpaid work equally. If you have a partner who doesn't respond in the right way to this, you need to ask some serious questions about your relationship.

Get comfortable with self-marketing and making your work visible. Don't wait for your boss to notice all the great work you are doing 'under the umbrella' or get frustrated that your male colleagues get more face time. Accept that, no matter how good a manager you have, he isn't going to spend his whole day thinking about you and your work. Help him out, help him to see you.

Networking isn't a crime; get comfortable with it. 'Relationship currency' is as important as 'performance currency' when it comes to decisions about jobs and promotions and when you need a relationship, it may be too late to build it. Spending time on building relationships is not a waste of time and you need to find room for it in your busy day – and learn how to have networking discussions and talk about your career aspirations in a way that is natural for you.

Remember it's not personal, it's work. Don't get emotionally attached. It's a job contract, it's a company – it's not your family and it's not your friend.

Stop accepting a lower salary than your male peers. Don't allow this to happen when you are as competent and working as hard. Value yourself and show that you do. Find a way that works for you to discuss your salary with your boss. Some women write an email because it feels less awkward and embarrassing – but find a way. Yes, you should be able to rely on your manager or company to be paying you fairly but, at least for now, I'm afraid you can't.

Be proactive and take ownership of your career. It is yours to own, nobody else's, so don't be a victim, and take responsibility. Do lay out what you would like from your career and do protest if you don't get the job or promotion you feel you deserve – if necessary, show you value yourself and vote with your feet and leave (this is what men do and it shows they value themselves and this makes others value them). And get yourself out of a role if it is not for you and get into one that is; as Dame Cilla Snowball says, 'Choose the right place to work and the right people to work with.' Find a place that fits you, not a place you have to fit into. Being in a place where you feel you belong and can be your authentic self is everything and you will not ultimately succeed without this.

Lead like a woman. In the words of Lord Browne, former CEO of BP, 'women don't have to be honorary men'.[23] Don't try to 'fit in' and copy men and act like they do – women copying men is not the answer, it's not authentic, it isn't you. People will feel it and it will make them trust you less. Know your strengths and leverage them. Be yourself. Go all in on you and lead as yourself – it's the only way you will ultimately succeed, not just in the big job but admired in the job and thus laying the pathway for more brilliant and authentic women to follow you. The only way we will truly become equal is by staying authentic, which means staying different.

Lead like a woman in meetings. Do it your way. You don't need to hurry; you are entitled to take the time you need to convey your message and ensure it hits home, but you don't need to copy the way men 'give good meeting'. Share of voice (SOV) is not equal to share of impact (SOI). In fact, Fama Francisco believes that 'SOI is inversely proportional to SOV' and impact comes in many forms – there is huge power in succinctness and clarity, so use it with confidence.

Be proud to say you are a feminist. Stop colluding with men on this, stop trying to be 'one of them' and to fit in by avoiding saying you are a feminist.

You are reinforcing a false and damaging image of what it means, and negating the experience of other women and betraying them. Sophie Walker, previous leader of the Women's Equality Party, says that 'If one woman's body is for sale, every woman's body is for sale'. Well, we can also say that if one woman is treated unequally, every woman is. Remember the simple definition of feminism: the belief in the social, political and economic equality of the sexes. Educate people, men and women, who resist feminism and remind them of the definition. Be proud to tell them you are a feminist and challenge them on why they are not a feminist too.

Make the sisterhood a reality and support other women. Don't see your peers and younger, up and coming women as competition; think of their victory as your victory. Mentor them but go further and sponsor them too. Don't let men get the jobs and promotions women deserve, stick your neck out and recommend them. Remember Madeleine Albright's 'There's a special place in hell for women who don't help other women'? I prefer Forbes' recent take on it: 'There is a special place in heaven for women who support other women.'[24] Coach and teach them. Tell them how things work, give them advice on how to manage all the unconscious dynamics while staying authentically themselves. Prepare them for the Invisible Ceiling – because if we make them aware of it, we empower them to push through it.

Men

I'm ending with my To Do list for men because you are ultimately the most important audience for this book. Without you, it doesn't matter what women do. Without you, nothing can change. In the words of Laurence Comte-Arassus, President of Meditronic France (who in 2018 set the goal of having women representing 40% of their management), 'L'impératif est de faire comprendre que la parité n'est pas un sujet de femmes.'[25] (which translates as 'The important thing to understand is that equality is not a woman's issue.') This needs to be a team effort and this means we need you to embrace the cause – and fully. In the words of Laura Bates, 'You're either with us or you're against us. There is no in-between... sitting on the fence is turning a blind eye... We need you. We need you to stand with us. And we can't do it without you.'[26] First and foremost, we need you to acknowledge this is still a huge issue and not go along with the popular but frankly incorrect view that we're making good progress. You wouldn't tell a black man that there is no racism issue in the world anymore, so don't tell a woman (or anyone, for that matter) that there is no sexism. Acknowledge it and understand it, understand the invisible power of the male-dominant culture and don't allow it to govern your world or the world around you. 'Learn to notice your privilege and use it honourably' as the MARC training teaches. And remember, supporting gender equality is a huge sign of strength and confidence in a man. As Ben Bailey Smith (Doc Brown) says, only 'weak men prey on the vulnerable'.[27] At one level, this should be very natural for a man to do. All you need to do is bring the support you have for the women and girls you love at home to work. In the words of Dr Michael Kimmel, 'All men know what it feels like to love women and want them to thrive.'[28]

So if you're ready for this, here's your To Do list:

Be an open supporter of women. Be the person in the meeting who speaks up for women Don't underestimate how important your support is. It is more convincing and an enormous help when you back us. When you see sexist behaviour, say 'that's not cool'. When you see gender inequality in a decision, ask 'Why?' When you champion this cause, we unite.

Ban the B word. Stop using words like 'bossy', 'pushy' or 'painful' about women that you wouldn't use about men. Words like these diminish women and can make them withdraw and hold back. Why would you want to do that?

Watch your own behaviour in meetings and, when you run them, do it in a way that gets women to contribute. Don't let the men dominate the airtime and interrupt. Go back to the woman who was making a point and say, 'You were interrupted'. Be aware that women may find it difficult to cut in and will generally wait for an appropriate opportunity to speak. Find a way to enable that.

Sponsor women. I know many men are feeling nervous now about being alone with a woman they work with for fear of a false sexual harassment claim against them and yes, it unfortunately does happen in some rare cases. But so unfortunately do false date rape accusations and it doesn't stop you going out on dates does it? So please, don't use it as an excuse. Women need your sponsorship to get the big jobs and promotions, they can't do it with work and performance alone – you know that's not how it works. So, help them, just like you help the men.

 Paternity leave – take it! It is one of the single most important things we can do to drive gender equality. Encourage all the fathers you know to take it – and, above all, don't even think about making fun of them for doing it. The men who take full on paternity leave are heroes and are paving the way for gender equality in the future.

Do 50% of the work at home. Share the childcare and housework. The shopping, cooking, laundry, cleaning. That means the repetitive daily housework, not just the exceptional, heroic 'one time' things every now and again. And teach your sons to do the same. More Mexican women work than women of any other country – 94% versus the global average of 78% – and yet they report greater levels of satisfaction in nearly every aspect of their lives because they have more help at home, with husbands in Mexico shouldering more household chores than the global average. Sweden, where life expectancy is 83 years, has the highest percentage of household tasks carried out by both partners (versus 29% in the US and 26% in the UK).[29] Sharing the workload at home is possibly the most important thing you can do to enable the career of your significant female other – and to improve your relationship and your lives.

Be aware that you are unwittingly influenced by many unconscious and invisible things to believe that men are better. Know that you have many role models for strong male leaders but not many female ones (because there aren't many female ones yet), so you may not recognise or like it when a woman displays qualities that you accept in a man. Be aware that men are more comfortable in your culture than women are, and this makes them feel and seem more confident and authentic. But they are not better. You are missing out on brilliant female candidates for your jobs. Your company is missing out. Your results are missing out. You company is making less money than it could, which means you are making less money than you could. You are winning at work, but this is not a good thing. This is not a game you want to win because, in the long-term, this will make you lose. This is one game where the best result is a draw.

Be a male role model for gender diversity. Don't just understand it, don't just care about it, don't just go on the training course you were told you had to go on and feel like you have ticked the box. I hope you have understood from this book that this is a man's world – unconscious bias is on your side, you are the part of and comfortable in the dominant culture, you have a naturally stronger self-confidence and aura of leadership that comes with that, you are more comfortable pushing for career and salary progress and not disliked for it and, as a result of all this, you have virtually all of the top jobs in the world. You are winning at work. If you change nothing, you will keep promoting men like you ahead of very competent, talented women. It is that simple – men have the power to promote and so men, not women, have the power to change the gender profile at work. It is a man's world and we need men to help us change it – we simply cannot do this without men. If you do nothing, it will stay a man's world. Forever. I hope by now you are as convinced as I am that this isn't what you want.

I think we have learnt the hard way that it is not enough to not be racist: we need to be anti-racist. In the same way, it is not enough to simply not be sexist and think that is enough: we need you to be a feminist. And feminism is not something to dislike and distrust. Stop thinking of it as negative and threatening. Keep in mind one of my all-time favourite Pins: 'If you think women should have the same rights as men, you're a feminist. Seriously. You are. I'm sorry to be the bearer of bad news.'

So, go on, be a feminist. In fact, be a femanist. Be proud to say it, be proud to say that you want to see women getting the roles and promotions they deserve and not losing out because of their gender. And multiply yourself through others. That's it. That's where we need to start.

And then the hard work to make it happen begins.

Final word

I HOPE YOU are now a believer, if you weren't already, in the importance of driving gender equality and are ready to join me in this mission. Addressing this issue will help us all (not just the 50% of us that are women) in such far reaching ways. It will make our businesses perform better, our homes happier, our countries stronger. Once we see how powerful we can be when we leverage different ways of seeing and doing things, we will move forwards in all areas of diversity. We will stop wanting a male or white or heterosexual dominant culture because we will finally understand its limits. We will stop wanting one type of person to win at work because we will know this means we are not fielding the best team and that we are not as strong as we could be.

If you are ready to take this on with me – as a woman, man, business or organisation – please get in touch. You can find me at www.gillwhittycollins.com.

I'm standing ready to help.

Acknowledgements

Huge thanks to Jo Bougourd (née Scaife) and Francois Facomprez for being my 'design targets' and first 'torture test' readers. I knew that if I could persuade you, I can persuade anyone, and your encouragement and feedback gave me confidence when I most needed it.

To my son Joe Collins, for his 'eagle eye for editing' and, above all, for all the questions he asked and for the discussions we had that led to so many insights and mini epiphanies about men and women.

Thanks also to Diana Brush for your eagle eyes and Clare Grist Taylor for your invaluable and generous publishing advice.

And to Emma Miller, Jane Leah, Nicki Lundy, Michela Ratti, Srebi Hanak, Olesya Nazarova and Sofía Lahmann for your introductions and PR and marketing brilliance.

I also thank Sallie Peters and Colette Maguire at GALLUP® for their help and advice in authorising the reproduction of extracts from GALLUP® reports and websites in this book.

A huge thank you to all the contributors and especially to the Super 7% who gave their time to be interviewed by me, anonymously and otherwise – I hope this book plays a part in helping more like you rise and succeed.

Last but not least, to Nigel Davies for the brilliant cover design and to Maia Gentle, Carrie Hutchison, Jennie Renton, Gavin MacDougall and the whole team at Luath Press, who have been a joy to publish this book with.

Endnotes

PREFACE

1   unwomen.org – Facts and figures: Ending violence against women

CHAPTER 1

1   Toksvig, S, 2018, speech at Women's Equality Party Conference see also Toksvig, S, 2016, 'A political party for women's equality', TED, YouTube (online)

2   *Fortune*, 2020, 'Fortune 500: Explore the 500' (online)

3   Current statistics are maintained at: 'Women CEOs of the S&P 500', Catalyst (online)

4   GALLUP® Inc., 2016, 'Women in America: Work and Life Well-Lived' (online)

5   Coffman, J and Neuenfeldt, B, 2014, 'Everyday Moments of Truth: Frontline Managers Are Key to Women's Career Aspirations', Bain & Company (online)

6   Hampton-Alexander Review, November 2019, 'FTSE Women Leaders: Improving Gender Balance in FTSE Leadership'

7   'The Female FTSE Index' is published annually by Cranfield School of Management (online)

8   Huber, C and O'Rourke, S, 2017, 'How to Accelerate Gender Diversity on Boards', *McKinsey Quarterly*

9   Hunt, V et al, 2018, 'Delivering through Diversity', McKinsey & Company (online)

10   Grant Thornton, 2016, 'Women in Business: Turning Promise into Practice', Grant Thornton International Business Report 2016 (online)

11   Aram-Dixon, K et al, 2017, 'Alpha Female Report 2017', Citywire (online)

12   Varadan, M et al, 2019, 'Getting Rid of Gender Bias in Venture Capital', Economics & Finance Blog (online)

13   US Bureau of Labor Statistics, 2019, 'Report 1084: Women in the Labor Force: A Databook', United States Government (online)

14   United Nations, 2017, 'System-wide Strategy on Gender Parity' (online)

15   Current statistics are maintained at 'Facts and Figures: Leadership and Political Participation, Women in Parliaments', United Nations Women (online)

16 World Economic Forum, 2020, 'Mind the 100 Year Gap: Global Gender Gap Report 2020' (online)

17 UK Parliament, 2020, 'Women in Parliament and Government', House of Commons Library (online)

18 Bates, L, 2014, *Everyday Sexism,* Simon & Schuster UK, p.14

19 Ibid, p.66–7

20 World Economic Forum, 2020, 'Mind the 100 Year Gap: Global Gender Gap Report 2020' (online)

21 World Bank Group, 2020, 'Women, Business and the Law 2020' (online)

22 Bates, L, 2014, *Everyday Sexism,* Simon & Schuster UK, p.73

23 Bawdon, F, Martinson, J et al, 2012, 'Seen but not Heard: How Women Make Front Page News', Women in Journalism (online)

24 Bates, L, 2014, *Everyday Sexism,* Simon & Schuster UK, p.182

25 United Nations, 2020, 'Visualizing the Data: Women's Representation in Society' and *The Guardian,* 2020, 'The Oscars: The 92-year Gender Gap Visualized'

26 Smith, S, 2014, 'Gender in Media: The Myths and Facts', Geena Davis Institute on Gender in Media (online)

27 Geena Davis Institute on Gender in Media, 2017, 'The Geena Benchmark Report 2007–2017' (online)

28 Davis, G, 2019, 'What 2.7M YouTube Ads Reveal About Gender Bias in Marketing', Geena Davis Institute on Gender in Media (online)

29 The 30% Movement, 2016, 'What Women Want' (online)

30 Lam, O et al, 2018, 'Gender and Jobs in Online Image Searches', Pew Research Centre (online)

31 Van Dam, A, 2020, 'Google an Image of a Manager or CEO, and You're Almost Certain to See a Man', *The Washington Post* (online)

32 Jakobsdóttir, K, 2019, speech at the UN Annual Summit of Women Activists

33 Bates, L, 2014, *Everyday Sexism,* Simon & Schuster UK, p.206–207

34 Ibid., p.240

35 Silverstein, MJ and Sayre, K, 2009, *Women Want More: How to Capture Your Share of the World's Largest, Fastest-Growing Market,* Collins Business, p.220–228

36 Ibid., p.246

37 Liswood, LA, 2009, *The Loudest Duck: Moving Beyond Diversity while Embracing Differences to Achieve Success at Work,* Wiley

38 Gender Pay Gap in the UK, Office of National statistics www.ons.gov.uk

39 BBC, 2019, 'BBC Statutory Gender Pay Report 2019' (online)

40 ITN Gender and Ethnicity Pay Gap Report 2018–19 www.itn.co.uk

41 Zipkin, N, 2016, 'New Study Finds the Global Gender Pay Gap Won't Be Closed Until 2186', Entrepreneur Europe (online)

42 Eurostat Gender Pay Gap Statistics www.ec.europa.eu

43 *Les Echos Executives*, 2019, 'Féminisation: 7 Conseil pour Accélérer' (online)

44 US Bureau of Labor Statistics, 2019, 'Report 1083: Highlights of Women's Earnings in 2018', United States Government (online)

45 GALLUP® Inc., 2016, 'Women in America: Work and Life Well-Lived' (online)

46 *Nikkei Asian Review*, 2017, 'Japan's gender wage gap persists despite progress' (online)

47 Bates, L, 2014, *Everyday Sexism,* Simon & Schuster UK, p.240

48 Purcell, K et al, 2012, 'Futuretrack Stage 4: Transitions into Employment, Further Study and Other Outcomes', HECSU

49 Current statistics are maintained by the Office of National Statistics at 'Understanding the Gender Pay Gap in the UK', ONS (online)

50 Bates, L, 2014, *Everyday Sexism,* Simon & Schuster UK, p.182

51 The world billionaire statistics are published annually at forbes.com

52 Reported in 2014, techcrunch.com

53 Milkman, KL., Akinola, M, & Chugh, D, 2015, 'What Happens Before? A Field Experiment Exploring How Pay and Representation Differentially Shape Bias on the Pathway Into Organizations' in *Journal of Applied Psychology* (online)

54 Correll, SJ et al, 2007, 'Getting a Job: Is There a Motherhood Penalty?' in *American Journal of Sociology*, Vol. 112, No. 5 (online)

55 Ibid., p.46

CHAPTER 2

1 Ngozi Adichie, C, 2012, 'We should all be feminists', TED, YouTube (online)

2 Morrissey, H, 2018, *A Good Time to be a Girl*, William Collins

3   Hekman, DR, Johnson, SK, Foo, M and Yang, W, 2016, 'Does Diversity-Valuing Behavior Result in Diminshed Performance Ratings for Nonwhite and Female Leaders?', Gender Action Portal, Harvard Kennedy School

4   Morrissey, H, 2018, *A Good Time to be a Girl*, William Collins

5   Bates, L, 2014, *Everyday Sexism,* Simon & Schuster UK, p.64

6   Ibid, p.109–110

7   Ibid, p.218

8   Davis, M, 2018, 'Eibar: The Female President & Football Philosophy Behind Real Madrid Conquerors', BBC Sport (online)

9   Bates, L, 2014, *Everyday Sexism,* Simon & Schuster UK, p.15

10   Chira, S, 2017, 'Why Women Aren't CEOs, According to Women Who Almost Were', *The New York Times* (online)

CHAPTER 3

1   Bates, L, 2014, *Everyday Sexism,* Simon & Schuster UK, p.34

2   Rumsfeld, D, 1962, 'Unknown unknowns', YouTube (online)

3   Allassan, F, 2019, '63% of Directors Say Investors Pay Too Much Attention to Corporate Board Gender Diversity', Axois (online)

4   Price Waterhouse Cooper, 2019, 'The Collegiality Conundrum: Finding Balance in the Boardroom' (online)

5   www.michaelkimmel.com/biography

6   Ibid.

7   OECD, 2019, 'Better Life Index: Sweden' (online)

8   United Nations Women, 2019, 'Map: Women in Politics' (online)

9   Silverstein, MJ and Sayre, K, 2009, *Women Want More: How to Capture Your Share of the World's Largest, Fastest-Growing Market*, Collins Business, p.204

10   Hunt, V et al, 2018, 'Delivering through Diversity', McKinsey & Company (online)

11   Woetzel, J et al, 2015, 'How Advancing Women's Equality Can Add \$12 Trillion to Global Growth', McKinsey Global Institute (online)

12   Sandi Toksvig, 2018, speech at Women's Equality Party Conference

13   Silverstein, MJ and Sayre, K, 2009, *Women Want More: How to Capture Your Share of the World's Largest, Fastest-Growing Market*, Collins Business, p.300

14 Smith, F, 2016, 'Privilege is invisible to those who have it', *The Guardian* (online)
15 Goldman Sachs, 'Insights' (online)
16 WGEA, Bankwest Curtin Economics Centre
17 Carter, NM, and Wagner, HM, 2011, 'The Bottom Line: Corporate Performance and Women's Representation on Boards (2004–2008)', Catalyst (online)
18 Thriving Talent, 2019, 'The Business Case for Diversity & Inclusion' (online)
19 Iritani, E, 2005, 'Fostering Good Will with Jobs', *Los Angeles Times*
20 Hunt, V et al, 2018, 'Delivering through Diversity', McKinsey & Company (online)
21 Badal, S, 2014, 'The Business Benefits of Gender Diversity', GALLUP® Inc. (online)
22 Abbatiello, A et al, 2018, 'Inclusive Leadership: Unlocking the Value of Diversity and Inclusion', Russell Reynolds Associates https://www.russellreynolds.com/insights/thought-leadership
23 Woolley, A and Malone, T, 'Defend Your Research: What Makes a Team Smarter? More Women' in *Harvard Business Review* 89(6):32–3 (online)
24 Ibid.
25 Ibid.
26 Quiles, E, 2019, '*Féminisation: 7 conseils pour accélérer*' in *Les Echos Executive*, 2019
27 Page, S, 2008, *The Difference: How the Power of Diversity Creates Better Groups, Firms, Schools and Societies*, Princeton University Press, p.370
28 Haldane, A, 2016, 'The Sneetches', Bank of England (online)

CHAPTER 4
1 College Factual, 2018, 'Admissions Statistics' (online)
2 Borzelleca, D, 2012, 'The Male-Female Ratio in College', Forbes (online)
3 Ratcliffe, R, 2013, 'The Gender Gap at Universities: Where Are All the Men?', *The Guardian* (online)
4 Statista, 2020, 'Number of Bachelor's Degrees Earned in the United States' (online)
5 Current statistics are maintained at 'SAT Program participation and performance statistics', CollegeBoard (online)
6 Chira, S, 2017, 'Why Women Aren't CEOs, According to Women Who Almost Were', *The New York Times* (online)
7 Friedberg, B, 2019, 'Why Smart Investors Should Check Out

These Women-Led Companies', The Balance (online)

8   Ozanian, M, 2010, 'Girls Rule', Forbes (online)

9   Desvaux, G et al, 2007, 'Women Matter', McKinsey & Company (online)

10   Konrad, A, 2015, 'VC Firm First Round: Our Female Founders Outshine the Men', Forbes (online)

11   Zenger, J and Folkman, J, 2019, 'Research: Women Score Higher Than Men in Most Leadership Skills' in *Harvard Business Review* (online)

12   Ibid.

13   GALLUP® Inc., 2016, 'Women in America: Work and Life Well-Lived' (online)

14   Ibid.

15   Chattopadhyay, R and Duflo, E, 2004, 'Women as Policy Makers: Evidence from a Randomized Policy Experiment in India' in Econometrica, Vol. 72 No. 5 (online)

16   Silverstein, MJ and Sayre, K, 2009, *Women Want More: How to Capture Your Share of the World's Largest, Fastest-Growing Market*, Collins Business, p.241

17   Chamorro-Premuzic, T, 'Why Do So Many Incompetent Men Become Leaders?', TEDx Talks: University of Nevada, YouTube (online)

18   Lewis, H, 6 May 2020, 'The Pandemic Has Revealed the Weakness of Strongmen', in *The Atlantic* (online)

19   Banaji, M, 2014, *Blindspot: Hidden Biases of Good People*, Penguin UK

20   Liswood, LA, 2009, *The Loudest Duck*, Wiley

21   Ibid.

CHAPTER 5

1   The MARC Program is a series of workshops run by global non-profit Catalyst

2   Bates, L, 2014, *Everyday Sexism*, Simon & Schuster UK, p.162

3   Ibid, p.203–4

4   Smith, F, 2016, 'Privilege is Invisible to Those Who Have it', *The Guardian* (online)

5   Liswood, LA, 2009, *The Loudest Duck*, Wiley

6   Dublin, D, 2017, quoted in Lorman, S, 'Women at the Top of the Corporate Ladder Agree: It's Lonely Up There', www.thriveglobal.com

7   Liswood, LA, 2009, *The Loudest Duck*, Wiley

8   Kimmell, M, 2016, speech at International Gender Champions

Geneva

9   Liswood, LA, 2009, *The Loudest Duck*, Wiley
10   Ibid.
11   Sartre, J-P, 1943, 'Authenticity' in Stanford Encyclopaedia of
      Philosophy (online)
12   Thorpe-Moscon, J and Pollack, A, 2014, *Feeling Different:
      Being the 'Other' in US Workplaces*, Catalyst
13   Palmieri, J, 2018, 'An Open Letter to the Women Who Will
      Run the World', RSA Events, YouTube (online)
14   Scalzi, J, 2012, 'Straight White Male: The Lowest Difficulty
      Setting There Is', Whatever.Scalzi.com (online)
15   Burkhart, J, 2018, 'We're Half Blind Until We Work With the
      Unconscious', Medium.com (online)
16   Tarvis, C and Aronson, E, 2015, *Mistakes Were Made (But
      Not By Me!)*, Pinter Martin
17   Bohnet, I, 2016, *What Works: Gender Equality by Design*,
      Harvard Univeristy Press, p.40
18   Rice, C, 2013, 'How Blind Auditions Help Orchestras to
      Eliminate Gender Bias', *The Guardian* (online)
19   Bates, L, 2014, *Everyday Sexism*, Simon & Schuster UK, p.230
20   Riffkin, R, 2014, 'Americans Still Prefer a Male Boss to a
      Female Boss', GALLUP® Inc. (online)
21   Varadan, M et al, 2019, 'Getting Rid of Gender Bias in
      Venture Capital', Economics & Finance Blog (online)
22   Bates, L, 2014, *Everyday Sexism*, Simon & Schuster UK, p.225
23   Jung, C, 1970, *Collected Works of CG Jung*, Princeton
      University Press
24   Marilyn Monroe best quotes at Vogue (online)

CHAPTER 6

1   Baron-Cohen, S, 2007, 'Do Women Have Better Empathy than
      Men?', Edge video (online)
2   Brizendine, L, 2008, *The Female Brain*, Bantam
3   Ibid.
4   Kay, K and Shipman, C, 2014, 'The Confidence Gap', *The
      Atlantic* (online)
5   Coates, JM, and Herbert, J, 2008, 'Endogenous Steroids
      and Financial Risk Taking on a London Trading Floor',
      Proceedings of the National Academy of Sciences (online)
6   Brizendine, L, 2008, *The Female Brain*, Bantam
7   Estima, S, 2019, 'Decoding the Female Brain', KwikBrain
      Podcast 093 (online)

8   Brizendine, L, 2008, *The Female Brain*, Bantam
9   Bundel, A, 2018, 'A Famous Margaret Atwood Quote Made It Into 'The Handmaid's Tale', Elite Daily (online)
10   Vaughan, S, 2018, *Anatomy of a Scandal*, Simon & Schuster UK
11   Alderman, N, 2016, *The Power*, Viking

CHAPTER 7
1   Merriam-Webster.com Dictionary, 'Gravity', www.merriam-webster.com/dictionary/gravity
2   Adams, S, 2013, 'Your Voice Could Be Costing You Hundreds of Thousands of Dollars, Study Shows', Forbes (online)
3   Gardner, B, 2014, 'From Shrill Housewife to Downing Street: The Changing Voice of Margaret Thatcher', *The Telegraph*
4   Liswood, LA, 2009, *The Loudest Duck*, Wiley
5   Bates, L, 2014, *Everyday Sexism*, Simon & Schuster UK, p.69
6   Kay, K and Shipman, C, 2014, 'The Confidence Gap', *The Atlantic* (online)
7   Cohen, C, 2015, 'Imposter Syndrome: Why Do So Many Women Feel Like Frauds?', *The Telegraph*
8   Chira, S, 2017, 'Why Women Aren't CEOs, According to Women Who Almost Were', *The New York Times* (online)
9   Sandberg, S, 2013, *Lean In: Women, Work and the Will to Lead*, WH Allen
10   Bock, L, 2016, *Work Rules!: Insights from Inside Google That Will Transform How You Live and Lead*, John Murray
11   Fox, R and Lawless, J, 2010, 'If Only They'd Ask: Gender, Recruitment, and Political Ambition' in *The Journal of Politics*, 72:2
12   Davidson, M, 2009, 'Why XX must think like XY to earn more K', BBC News Magazine (online)
13   Babcock, L and Laschever, S, 2008, *Why Women Don't Ask*, Piatkus Books
14   Ehrlinger, J and Dunning, D, 2003, 'How Chronic Self-Views Influence (and Potentially Mislead) Estimates of Performance' in *Journal of Personality and Social Psychology*, Vol.84 No.1 (online)
15   Babcock, L and Laschever, S, 2008, *Why Women Don't Ask*, Piatkus Books
16   Kay, K and Shipman, C, 2014, 'The Confidence Gap', *The Atlantic* (online)
17   Bell, LA, 1990, 'The gifted woman as impostor' in Advanced Development, Vol. 2 (online)

18 Storr, F, 2018, *The Discomfort Zone: How to Get What You Want by Living Fearlessly*, Piatkus

19 Kay, K and Shipman, C, 2014, 'The Confidence Gap', *The Atlantic* (online)

20 Ibid.

21 Morrissey, H, 2018, *A Good Time to be a Girl*, William Collins

22 Inzlicht, M and Ben-Zeev, T, 2000, 'A Threatening Intellectual Environment: Why Females are Susceptible to Experiencing Problem-solving Deficits in the Presence of Males', in *Psychological Science*, Vol.11 No.5 (online)

23 Stanberry, K, 2012, 'Single-sex Education: The Pros and Cons', GreatSchools.org (online)

24 Sax, L et al, 2009, 'Women Graduates of Single-Sex and Coeducational High Schools: Differences in their Characteristics and the Transition to College', The Sudikoff Family Institute for Education & New Media / UCLA Graduate School of Education & Information Studies (online)

25 Dix, K, 2017, 'Single-sex Schooling and Achievement Outcomes', ACER Research Developments

26 Eisenkopf, G et al, 2015, 'Academic Performance and Single-sex Schooling: Evidence from a Natural Experiment in Switzerland', Gender Action Portal (online)

27 Bramley et al, 2015, 'Gender differences in GCSE', Cambridge Assessment Report

28 Park, H et al, 2012, 'Do Single-Sex Schools Enhance Students' Stem (Science, Technology, Engineering and Mathematics) Outcomes?', PIER Working Paper, No.12-038 (online)

29 Diaconu, D, 2012, 'Modelling Science Achievement Differences Between Single-sex and Coeducational Schools', eScholarship at Boston College (online)

30 See Professor Alison Booth's multiple publications at the Australian National University (online)

31 UK school league tables are published annually in *The Telegraph* (online)

32 Glass, A, 2013, 'Ernst & Young Studies The Connection Between Female Executives And Sports', Forbes (online)

33 'Kay, K and Shipman, C, May 2014, 'The Confidence Gap' in *The Atlantic* (online)

34 Bailey, R et al, 2002, 'Girls' Participation in Physical Activities and Sports, Patterns, Influences and Ways Forward', WHO (online)

35 Swiss Women Sports Survey, 2017, 'Ville de Genève Service des Sports Survey', University Bordeaux Montaigne

36 Storr, F, 2019, 'Why Imposter Syndrome is Every Woman's Secret Weapon', Elle.com (online)

37 Frankel, LP, 2014, *Nice Girls Don't Get The Corner Office: Unconscious Mistakes Women Make That Sabotage Their Careers*, Business Plus, p.185

38 Shemmer, M, 26 March 2019, 'Confidence is a Choice', Linkedin (online)

39 Collins, J, 2001, *Good to Great*, Random House Business

40 Chamorro-Premuzic, T, 'Why Do So Many Incompetent Men Become Leaders?', TEDx Talks: University of Nevada, YouTube (online)

41 Ibid.

42 Greig, F, 2008, 'Propensity to Negotiate and Career Advancement: Evidence from an Investment Bank that Women Are on a "Slow Elevator" in *Negotiation Journal*, Vol.24, No.4 (online)

43 Bohnet, I, 2016, *What Works*, Harvard Univeristy Press, p.189

CHAPTER 8

1 Neufeld, A, 2005, 'Costs of an Outdated Pedagogy? Study on Gender at Harvard Law School' in Journal of Gender, Social Policy and the Law, Vol.13, No.3 (online)

2 Gupta, AH, 14 April 2020, 'It's Not Just You: In Online Meetings, Many Women Can't Get a Word In', *New York Times* (online)

3 Liswood, LA, 2009, *The Loudest Duck*, Wiley

4 McKinsey & Company and Lean.InOrg, 2019, 'Women in America 2019', https://www.mckinsey.com

5 Svodoba, E, 2018, 'Ben Barres: A Transgender Scientist Shares His Story', Spectrum (online)

6 Mayrath, N, 2019, 'What Companies Can Do to Close the Gender Gap', Yahoo Finance (online)

CHAPTER 9

1 Harris, CA, 2014, *Strategize to Win: The New Way to Start Out, Step Up, or Start Over in Your Career*, Avery Publishing Group

2 Chira, S, 2017, 'Why Women Aren't CEOs, According to Women Who Almost Were', *The New York Times* (online)

3 Ibid.

4 Liswood, LA, 2009, *The Loudest Duck*, Wiley

5   GALLUP® Inc., 2016, 'Women in America: Work and Life Well-Lived' (online)
6   Liswood, LA, 2009, *The Loudest Duck*, Wiley
7   Ibid.
8   Giang, V, 2019, 'Most People are Focused on the Wrong Measure of Success', FastCompany (online)
9   Chira, S, 'Why Women Aren't CEOs, According to Women Who Almost Were', *New York Times* (online)
10 Harris, CA, 2014, *Strategize to Win*, Avery Publishing Group
11 US Bureau of Labor Statistics, 2019, 'American Time Use Survey – 2018 results', US Bureau of Labor (online)
12 Silverstein, MJ and Sayre, K, 2009, *Women Want More: How to Capture Your Share of the World's Largest, Fastest-Growing Market*, Collins Business, p.21
13 Current global statistics are maintained at Statista.com
14 www.leanin.org/article/women-shoulder-most-of-the-extra-work-because-of-covid-19
15 6 May 2020, 'Nearly Half of Men Say They Do Most of the Home-Schooling', *New York Times*
16 Miller, J and Adkins, A, 2016, 'Reality and Perception: Why Men Are Paid More', GALLUP® Inc. (online)
17 GALLUP® Inc., 2016, 'Women in America: Work and Life Well-Lived' (online)
18 www.ariannahuffington.com
19 Duke Medicine News, 2014, 'Stress May Be Harder on Women's Hearts than Men's', Duke University (online)
20 OneWorldNews, 2019, 'Everyday Gender Bias', online
21 GALLUP® Inc., 2016, 'Women in America: Work and Life Well-Lived' (online)
22 Estima, S, 21 June 2019, Instagram
23 GALLUP® Inc., 2016, 'Women in America: Work and Life Well-Lived' (online)
24 Wilson, H, 2019, 'The Millennial Dad at Work', Daddilife (online)
25 US Bureau of Labor Statistics, April 2020, 'Economic Situation Summary' (online)
26 GALLUP® Inc./International Labor Organization, 2017, 'Towards a Better Future for Women and Work: Voices of Women and Men' (online)
27 Hewlett, S, and Luce, CB, 2005, 'Off-Ramps and On-Ramps: Keeping Talented Women on the Road to Success' in *Harvard Business Review*, Vol.83, No.3 (online)

28 GALLUP® Inc./International Labor Organization, 2017,
    'Towards a Better Future for Women and Work: Voices of
    Women and Men' (online)
29 Current statistics are maintained by the Office of National
    Statistics at 'Understanding the Gender Pay Gap in the UK',
    ONS (online)
30 www.womendontask.com
31 Hewlett, S, and Luce, CB, 2005, 'Off-Ramps and On-Ramps:
    Keeping Talented Women on the Road to Success' in *Harvard
    Business Review*, Vol.83, No.3 (online)
32 Lartey, J, 5 September 2016, 'Women ask for pay increases as
    often as men but receive them less, study says', *The Guardian*

CHAPTER 10
1   Fortune, 2020, 'Fortune 500: Explore the 500'
2   Morrissey, H, 2018, *A Good Time to be a Girl*, William
    Collins
3   GALLUP® Inc., 2016, 'Women in America: Work and Life Well-
    Lived' (online)
4   Rath, T and Conchie, B, 2016, *Strengths-based Leadership*,
    GALLUP® Press, p.10
5   Ibid., p.10
6   Ibid.
7   Ibid., p.84
8   Silverstein, MJ and Sayre, K, 2009, *Women Want More:
    How to Capture Your Share of the World's Largest, Fastest-
    Growing Market*, Collins Business
9   Collins, J, 2001, *Good to Great*, Random House Business, p.20
10 Clifton, DO, and Harter, JK, 2003, 'Investing in Strengths', in
    Cameron, A et al (eds), *Positive Organizational Scholarship:
    Foundations of a New Discipline*, Berrett-Koehler Publishers,
    p.111–121
11 Rath and Conchie, Strengths Based Leadership, p.55
12 GALLUP®, 2016, 'Women in America: Work and Life Well-
    Lived' (online)
13 GALLUP® Inc., 2016, 'Women in America: Work and Life Well-
    Lived' (online)
14 From an interview with Edwina Dunne, hosted by AllBright
    on Instagram Live, 22 April 2020

CHAPTER 11
1   Groysberg, B, and Bell, D, 2013, 'Dysfunction in the

Boardroom: Understanding the Persistent Gender Gap at the Highest Levels' in *Harvard Business Review*, Vol.91, No.6 (online)

2   Albright, M, 2006, keynote speech at 'Celebrating Inspiration' luncheon with the WNBA's All-Decade Team

CHAPTER 12

1   Gray Scott, H, 2014, *Dare Mighty Things: Mapping the Challenges of Leadership for Christian Women*, Zondervan

2   Bagshawe, L, 2007, *Tall Poppies*, Headline Review

3   YouGov survey, 2016

4   Bohnet, I, 2016, *What Works*, Harvard Univeristy Press, p.22

5   Cope, R, 2018, '25 Celebrity Women on Gender Inequality in Hollywood', HarpersBazaar (online)

6   Bohnet, I, 2016, *What Works*, Harvard Univeristy Press, p.63

7   Yee, L et al, 2016, 'Women in the Workplace 2016', LeanIn. Org and McKinsey & Company (online)

8   Joyner, J, 5 March 2009, 'Palin Too Sexy for White House' in Outside the Beltway (online)

9   Bates, L, 2014, *Everyday Sexism*, Simon & Schuster UK, p.55

10   Forbes.com, 2016, 'Power Dressing: How Women Politicians Use Fashion' (online)

11   Brescoll, VL, 2011, 'Who Takes the Floor and Why' in *Administrative Science Quarterly*, Vol.56, No.4

12   Liswood, LA, 2009, *The Loudest Duck*, Wiley

13   Bates, L, 2014, *Everyday Sexism*, Simon & Schuster UK, p.60

14   Chira, S, 2017, 'Why Women Aren't CEOs, According to Women Who Almost Were, *The New York Times*

15   Brescoll, VL, 2011, 'Who Takes the Floor and Why' in *Administrative Science Quarterly*, Vol.56, No.4

16   Liswood, LA, 2009, *The Loudest Duck*, Wiley

17   Cooper, S, 2018, *How to Be Successful Without Hurting Men's Feelings*, Square Peg, p.5

18   Manning, S, 'Bloody Difficult Women' in *Red*, p.43

19   Ngozi Adichie, C, 2017, *Dear Ijeawele, or a Feminist Manifesto in Fifteen Suggestions*, Fourth Estate, p.36–39

CHAPTER 13

1   McKinsey.com

2   Morrissey, H, 2018, *A Good Time to be a Girl*, William Collins

3   Frankel, LP, 2014, *Nice Girls Don't Get The Corner Office*, Business Plus

4   BBC, 2019, *Andrew Marr Show*, BBC (online)
5   Bates, L, 2014, *Everyday Sexism*, Simon & Schuster UK, p.5

CHAPTER 14
1   Bohnet, I, 2016, *What Works*, Harvard Univeristy Press, p.50
2   Lorde, A, 1979, *The Master's Tools Will Never Dismantle the Master's House*, Penguin
3   President Espinosa, 2019, speech at Annual Summit of Women Activists at United Nations HQ
4   Sharma, SC, 2016, 'Women's Political Participation in India', Policy Perspectives (online)
5   Current statistics are maintained at IPU Parline, 'Global Data on National Parliaments' (online)
6   Bohnet, I, 2016, *What Works*, Harvard University Press, p.60
7   Vedantam, S, 2008, 'Most Diversity Training Ineffective, Study Finds', American Renaissance (online)
8   Dobbin, F and Kalev, A, 2014, 'Engaging, Instead of Blaming, Managers', *The New York Times* (online)
9   Morrissey, H, 2018, *A Good Time to be a Girl*, William Collins
10   Stillman, J, 2018, 'Michelle Obama Just Said, "Lean In" Doesn't Work', inc.com (online)
11   Frankel, LP, 2014, *Nice Girls Don't Get The Corner Office*, Business Plus
12   Bates, L, 2014, *Everyday Sexism*, Simon & Schuster UK, p.59
13   Liswood, LA, 2009, *The Loudest Duck*, Wiley

TO DO LISTS
1   Silverstein, MJ and Sayre, K, 2009, *Women Want More*, Collins Business, p.209
2   Bates, L, 2014, *Everyday Sexism*, Simon & Schuster UK, p.58
3   www.jane.org
4   Bohnet, I, 2016, *What Works*, Harvard University Press, p.4
5   Abbatiello, A et al, 2018, 'Inclusive Leadership: Unlocking the Value of Diversity and Inclusion', Russell Reynolds Associates (online)
6   Banks, I, 2013, *The Business*, Abacus
7   Knowledge@Wharton, 2012, 'The Vicious Cycle of the Gender Pay Gap', University of Pennsylvania (online)
8   Khomami, N and Treanor, J, 2017, 'BBC Women Let Pay Gap Happen', *The Guardian* (online)
9   Tanaka, S and Waldfogel, J, 2007, 'Effects of Parental Leave

and Work Hours on Fathers' Involvement with their Babies: Evidence from the Millennium Cohort Study' in *Community, Work and Family,* 10:4, p.409–26

10 US Department of Labor, 2016, 'Why Parental Leave for Fathers is so Important for Working Families' (online)

11 Patnaik, E, 2010, 'The Effect of Own and Spousal Parental Leave on Earnings' in Institute for Labour Market Policy Evaluation Working Paper, 2010:4

12 US Department of Labor, 2016, 'Why Parental Leave for Fathers is so Important for Working Families' (online)

13 Hampton-Alexander Review, 'FTSE Women Leaders'

14 GALLUP® Inc, 2016, 'Women in America: Work and Life Well-Lived' (online)

15 GALLUP®, 2016, 'Women in America: Work and Life Well-Lived' (online)

16 Ibid.

17 Morrissey, H, 2018, *A Good Time to be a Girl*, William Collins

18 Liswood, L.A, 2009, *The Loudest Duck*, Wiley

19 Bohnet, I, 2016, *What Works*, Harvard Univeristy Press, p.208

20 Kurtulus, FA and Tomaskovic-Devey, D, 2011, 'Do Woman Top Managers Help Women Advance?', Economics Department Working Paper Series, 122

21 McGinn, K and Milkman, K, 2013, 'Looking Up and Looking Out: Career Mobility Effects of Demographic Similarity among Professionals' in *Organization Science*, Vol.24, No.4

22 Roosevelt, E, 1940, *Sitka Sentinel*

23 Lord Browne, 2015, speech at 30% Club & OUTstanding event

24 Zalis, S, 2019, 'Power of the Pack: Women Who Support Women Are More Successful', Forbes (online)

25 *Les Echos Executives*, 2019, 'Féminisation: 7 conseil pour accélérer'

26 Bates, L, 2014, *Everyday Sexism,* Simon & Schuster UK, p.379–80

27 Mis, M (2014), 'British Rapper Calls Out Men to Stand Up for Women's Rights', Thomson Reuters Foundation (online)

28 Kimmel, M and Wade, L, 2018, 'Ask a Feminist: Michael Kimmel and Lisa Wade Discuss Toxic Masculinity', Signs (online)

29 Current global statistics are maintained at Statista.com

Please note that the quotes from the Super 7% women were shared directly with the author in interview.

Book group discussion points

What will you think when you next see that women have 30% of Company Board or Executive Committee positions?

What do you say if you are asked if you are a feminist or if you are a champion of gender equality?

Are your business or team's results as strong as they could be? Could a lack of gender diversity be holding you back from performing better?

Have you ever questioned if a woman has been appointed to a role because of merit or because of positive discrimination, even if the team she was joining was still male-dominated? Have you ever questioned the merit of a man who was appointed to a role in a male-dominated team?

When you think of the people who you think of as the best performers, are they similar to most of the other people in the team, or are they in a minority group?

Do you find yourself admiring men who are not afraid to take risks?
Have you looked at the data and benchmarked their performance and results versus other people on the team?

Think of the women you work with, or who work for you. How confident are they in communicating their point of view, or when answering a question about their work? Does this affect how you perceive their competence or contribution?

Have you ever noticed a woman being interrupted in a meeting, or her point being ignored?

Did you notice how she responded to this?
What will you do the next time you notice this?

Does your workplace have parental policies that are truly
equal for women and men?
How can we make it as easy and accepted for a man to take
parental leave or work flexible hours as it is for a woman?

Think of a female leader that you respect and admire. What
differentiates her for you from other female leaders that you
admire less?

Have you ever come across a successful female leader who
doesn't 'put the ladder' down for other women below her, or
even prefers to work with and support men?
Why do you think this is the case?

Have you ever called or thought of a woman bossy, pushy, or
too aggressive?
Can you remember what she said?
Have you ever heard a man say something similar and did
you have the same reaction?

Are you convinced that gender equality is still a key issue?
Do you agree that men win at work – and that you don't
think this is a good thing?
Are you ready to join the fight to make gender inequality
history?

Some useful organisations & web resources

Advance (Gender Equality in Business) www.weadvance.ch

AllBright www.allbrightcollective.com

Empower Women www.empowerwomen.org

European Women's Lobby www.womenlobby.org

Fawcett Society www.fawcettsociety.org.uk

Femmes Chefs D'Entreprises Mondiales www.fcem.org/en

50:50 The Equality Project www.bbc.co.uk/5050

Global Institute for Women's Leadership www.kcl.ac.uk/giwl

HeForShe heforshe.org

Global Women's Institute globalwomensinstitute.gwu.edu

Organisation of Women in International Trade www.owit.org

Our World in Data (Economic inequality by gender) www.ourworldindata.org/economic-inequality-by-gender

Revival Sanctuary www.revivalsanctuary.co.uk

SmartWorks www.smartworks.org.uk

The Circle www.thecircle.ngo

The Female Lead www.thefemalelead.com

UN Women www.unwomen.org

Women for Women International www.womenforwomen.org.uk

Wonder Foundation www.wonderfoundation.org.uk

Womankind Worldwide www.womankind.org.uk

Women's Aid www.womensaid.org.uk

Young Women's Trust www.youngwomenstrust.org

In support of

women's aid
until women & children are safe

Registered Charity No: 1054154

Thank you for reading this book. For every copy sold I will make a donation to the charity Women's Aid.

I am lucky to have been a witness only to 'luxury gender issues' and, while we must continue to fight the visible and invisible problems that are the subject of this book until we achieve true gender equality, let us not forget that there are women in the world facing a much more tangible fight. Supporting and protecting them must be our highest priority.

Women's Aid is a federation of over 180 organisations working to end domestic abuse – 1.4 million women per year experience abuse and three women a fortnight are killed by their male partner or former partner. Domestic abuse has escalated further since Covid-19.

You can make a donation at www.womensaid.org.uk

Gill Whitty-Collins

Luath Press Limited

mmitted to publishing well written books worth reading

UATH PRESS takes its name from Robert Burns, whose little collie Luath (*Gael.*, swift or nimble) tripped up Jean Armour at a wedding and gave him the chance to speak to the woman who was to be his wife and the abiding love of his life. Burns called one of the 'Twa Dogs' Luath after Cuchullin's hunting dog in Ossian's *Fingal*.
Luath Press was established in 1981 in the heart of Burns country, and is now based a few steps up the road from Burns' first lodgings on Edinburgh's Royal Mile. Luath offers you distinctive writing with a hint of unexpected pleasures.
Most bookshops in the UK, the US, Canada, Australia, New Zealand and parts of Europe, either carry our books in stock or can order them for you. To order direct from us, please send a £sterling cheque, postal order, international money order or your credit card details (number, address of cardholder and expiry date) to us at the address below. Please add post and packing as follows: UK – £1.00 per delivery address; overseas surface mail – £2.50 per delivery address; overseas airmail – £3.50 for the first book to each delivery address, plus £1.00 for each additional book by airmail to the same address. If your order is a gift, we will happily enclose your card or message at no extra charge.

Luath Press Limited
543/2 Castlehill
The Royal Mile
Edinburgh EH1 2ND
Scotland
Telephone: +44 (0)131 225 4326 (24 hours)
Email: sales@luath.co.uk
Website: www.luath.co.uk